IN DEFENSE OF LOOSE TRANSLATIONS

American Indian Lives

SERIES EDITORS

Kimberly Blaeser
University of Wisconsin, Milwaukee

Brenda J. Child
University of Minnesota

R. David Edmunds
University of Texas at Dallas

K. Tsianina Lomawaima
Arizona State University

IN DEFENSE
OF LOOSE
TRANSLATIONS

An Indian Life in an Academic World

Elizabeth Cook-Lynn

University of Nebraska Press | Lincoln and London

B
Cook-Lynn,
Elizabeth

Library of Congress Cataloging-in-Publication Data
Names: Cook-Lynn, Elizabeth, author.
Title: In defense of loose translations: an Indian life in a mainstream academic world / Elizabeth Cook-Lynn.
Other titles: American Indian lives.
Description: Lincoln: University of Nebraska Press, [2018] | Series: American Indian lives | Includes bibliographical references.
Identifiers: LCCN 2018008995
ISBN 9781496208873 (cloth: alk. paper)
ISBN 9781496212368 (epub)
ISBN 9781496212375 (mobi)
ISBN 9781496212382 (pdf)
Subjects: LCSH: Cook-Lynn, Elizabeth. | Indian authors—Biography. | Indian college teachers—Biography. | Indian activists—Biography. | LCGFT: Autobiographies.
Classification: LCC PS3553.O5548 Z46 2018 | DDC 818/.5409 [B]—dc23 LC record available at https://urldefense.proofpoint.com/v2/url?u=https-3a__lccn.loc.gov_2018008995&d=Dwifag&c=Cu5g146wZdoqVuKptnsyhefx_rg6kWhlklf8Eft-wwo&r=Qxk-cj_QrVzF1u7b7vxqTw&m=J2I3wkb9effrczqdsW_5Jswxk5ctixjgbNexm5nazwk&s=nDloaxmqu25ihfszzrm2gHezlxxgwngtqucIOpUr3Gk&e=

Set in Merope Basic by Mikala R Kolander.

Frontispiece: Old trail sign. Photo courtesy of Mary A. Cook. From the author's collection.

Illustrations

IN DEFENSE OF LOOSE TRANSLATIONS

PROLOGUE

I WAS BORN IN the country of the tall grass near Fort Thompson, South Dakota, in November 1930, just when the political conversations seeking home rule began on the Crow Creek Indian Reservation, just before the snow started to fall, and just as the 1934 Reorganization Act was passed by the U.S. Congress. I tell my students, "When you get as old as the IRA, hey . . . you've got some kind of perspective!"

It's a long way from the old Indian trails to modern America, yet these trails are the forerunners of all journeys traveled by the trespassers, who often point in troubling directions. New wisdom often focuses on the bystanders.

As soon as I learned to read English, I wanted to write. It took me years to use English well and to become a lover of poetry, which I eventually abandoned in order to become a vehement critic of apartheid, genocide, and the history of colonization that has kept entire societies enslaved. I've never belonged to clandestine organizations, nor have I been arrested or convicted of any crime, but my work has always been an attempt to continue the political insurrection of those who knew the old trails.

My only collection of poems was called *I Remember the Fallen Trees* (Eastern Washington University Press, 1998), the title a reference to the destruction of the Missouri River, one of the many large natural streams known to the Dakotas, sacrificed for twentieth-century fantasies of wealth. Another scar. Another wound. I don't do poetry anymore, but have come to believe that the revival and enrichment of forgotten memories may be the best revenge.

When I began to write this manuscript, I recognized my aesthetic positions about politics and language and tried to juxtapose the "civilizing mission" of being an American scholar with the voicelessness and facelessness of many of the tribal interests that swept me up in my youth.

I began with this question: *Is this a memoir?* As I went from that question into the remembrances of the years of my recent academic past, I realized the benefit of seeking inspiration from what might be called my intellectual and political priorities: those things that have been a truly critical force in a long and satisfying writer's life, the things that have led me into a profession as a speaker and writer of English, as well as a teacher, poet, declaimer, and writer of about a dozen books. Not the Dead Sea Scrolls, perhaps, but an addition to the canon formation of a scholarly and critical body of American Indian contemporary thought. Any exposés here, then, will appear in that context. The need to unfold history has been, for me, a way to grasp incongruities. Even so, you often hear me say, "there are no two sides to this history."

1

I HAVE KNOWN FROM the beginning that all of the places, voices, and ideas of my self and being would be held in language. I grew up with two languages and then went to a boarding school where the Mass was still offered in Latin. It is true that all the things my people (called the Sioux by their enemies) remembered about their times of glory were held in language, both Dakota and English. Many of the things they remembered about their times of grievance were held in English. This meant, for me, that I had to become a proficient user of the instruments and strategies of language if I were to be something other than a ghost or a shell.

I knew from the beginning, when I was a child of silence, that this road would not be easy and that it would, of necessity, leave many scars. Becoming a public voice is not now and was not, even in the beginning, a virtue to be sought by this youngest daughter of the Dakota Sioux traditions. Indeed, such a notion would have been absurd. But in many ways, this absurdity influences my tone of sarcasm, irony, satire. One of my first books was, after all, a brief little treatise on *Why I Can't Read Wallace Stegner*. How about that for a writer hesitant about claiming a Western voice?

Because of my interest in writing, then, it should not be thought unusual that I have not published anything in the Dakota language. The language of my grandmothers remains a language I can hardly read or write. I know it and hear it, often thinking about it in terms of unspeakable loneliness: *ohanh . . . Dakota iyapi tawahinda.*

3

But it is not a written language to me. Perhaps an astonishing revelation is that I did not publish anything until I was forty years old, and when I began, it was as a writer of works in English. I think of my use of English as an attempt toward usefulness and clarity, without nostalgia or legend.

Since then I've published several collections. I suppose most people of the academic world, if they think of my work at all, would think of it as being a part of the Cultural Left. What emerges is a rather snotty examination of the way narratives of scholarship meet up with how we want to rethink and rearticulate the very nature of disciplines. I transgressed disciplinary boundaries during my professing years, until I finally and with some regret flung myself out of contemporary English departments into politics and law and Native American/indigenous studies. The existing state of indifference by traditional American disciplines to the Indian historical perspective had become intolerable.

I do want to say here that, having navigated the imponderable possibilities as an indigenous person in America's colonial academic world, as all foreigners have, I realized I ought not take myself too seriously. If language is to function, we've got to mistrust it. That means there are two necessities for the following narratives: a slight wit . . . and, more, judgment.

2

I WAS AN ASSISTANT professor at Eastern Washington University when, in 1974, I was accepted as a fellow to study with Ian Watt at Stanford in an all-too-brief summer session of a National Humanities seminar called "Historical and Cultural Perspectives of Literary Criticism." This was before I had tenure and before I started working on a PhD at the University of Nebraska, Lincoln.

With great enthusiasm, I drove my overloaded amber-colored Pontiac from Cheney, Washington, to Palo Alto, California, with my eldest daughter, and we hurriedly rented (in the dead of night) a little apartment that had a "for rent" sign in the window.

Always loathe to make advance travel plans, we had been driving down the coast for hours and were thoroughly exhausted, which is a condition for making bad decisions. Among the many things we didn't know was that the apartment we rented was located within seeing distance of the Bay Area Rapid Transit station (BART), and a train roared past every hour, every day, including Saturdays and Sundays, taking sleepless San Franciscans south until after midnight.

The other thing we didn't know was that two adjoining apartments were occupied by a cadre of friendly and happy Hasidic Jews who danced and sang every night, celebrating the flowing of the wine to the accompaniment of a remarkable variety of instruments and clapping of hands. They never invited us to join them, and we were grateful for their exclusiveness. Thinking back on it, I am envious of a people who know that there should be more music in everybody's life, but at that time getting some sleep was, for us, a challenge.

Years before this seminar, I had tried to read *Ulysses* by James Joyce and was now becoming interested in the Joycean notion Watt expressed when we took up his text *The Rise of the Novel* (University of California Press, 1957, a bit dated, yes?). The notion was that the novel as genre mostly concentrated on private experiences and personal relationships. Joyce, as you may know, had also expressed his fondness for this trait in fiction. This focus had always seemed so different from the Dakota Sioux literary tradition of storytelling that I had come to know and may account for the fact that even today I seldom read contemporary fiction. Dakota stories seldom say, "I am a great man. Look at me." More often they say, "We are a great people." Generally speaking, then, I prefer historical narratives that take into account something other than a description of the inner lives of characters.

During the early days of my professorship at Eastern, I'd had the great luck to occupy an office in the English department next-door to a James Joyce specialist who helped me through some of it in our casual hallway conversations. Joyce always seemed to me to be an Irish writer who was colonized by the British and was enamored of what I called "the quest stuff." His heroes always accomplished some kind of victory, which is a trait, it seems to me, of imperial fiction, even though Joyce was probably more aware than most of how the so-called empire bumped up against what he thought of as the Irish sensibility. Some critics of the Joyce oeuvre suggest that when you have the feeling (or hidden hope?) that England's empire might be in danger, you turn to art. Joyce certainly thought of himself as an artist. Even history becomes suspect.

But Joyce was not what brought me to Ian Watt. What really interested me in Professor Watt was that he had written an essay on how historical event becomes myth. It was entitled "The Humanities on the River Kwai," and I had happened upon it years prior in my eclectic habit of reading everything in history and myth that I could get my hands on, the mythic essences of rivers always on my mind.

The essay had come late in Watt's writing and teaching career, after he had produced distinguished studies in the eighteenth-century fiction he loved talking about. Incessantly, he would go on and on during our symposium about the minutia of the bourgeois lives of the characters in *Howard's End*. Eyes glazed over in near ecstasy, he would come back to our presence from his musings with the phrase, "well, be that as it may." He would then launch into our next writing assignment.

The Watt essay in question, on how history becomes myth, had settled itself in the broader political experience in fiction and was what I was eager to know more about. He also wrote an engaging piece called "The Consequences of Literacy," a subject in anthropological studies that seemed to me a fruitful exploration for literature and history professors to examine.

Mostly, Watt's lectures were about Victorian literatures, but during the one lecture period when he talked about the "Kwai" essay, he told us that this little essay had come about because he, Ian Watt, the quintessential Englishman now teaching at such esteemed places as the Sorbonne in France and Stanford University in the United States, had been one of the British officers in a Japanese concentration camp during World War II, circa 1945. As a captured prisoner of war, he and others had begun building for the Japanese Imperial Army a wartime bridge through Thailand to Burma. It is today called the Thailand-Burma Railway bridge, and I understand it has now become a great curiosity to tourists.

Ten years after Watt left the POW camp, the story was fictionalized by the Frenchman Pierre Boulle in a novel called *The Bridge on the River Kwai*, and ten years after that it became a splendid movie of the same name starring William Holden. This, I thought then, was an example of how a historical event becomes myth.

I think I was always a little intimidated by the new academic world into which I had stumbled, and especially when we were invited to the professor's place in the Palo Alto Hills, far from the madding crowd.

I forged ahead with anticipation even though I could not conceive of what I had in common with everyone there. Symposium attendees crowded into a van, and a couple of us drove our own cars, following closely behind. Into the Palo Alto Hills we went. My aging Pontiac had never seen the likes of this!

We drove past the mansions of people such as the president of the Bank of America and Joan Baez, with me mumbling to myself about the immutable nature of this world as distinguished from the places where the small and insignificant Indian villagers of South Dakota resided. Such opulence! The broadest roads and driveways in the known world! Stone houses lined with glass windows. Where has the prairie gone? And the meandering creeks and the toads in the pasture dam?

It was early in the day with pop songs from my car radio already dominating the cool air. Songs about parking lots replacing paradise were cheerful renditions of the dismal thoughts so notable on the pop music scene at the moment. I was looking forward to what I was sure would be a luxurious luncheon. It was an upbeat morning!

When we stepped into the doorway of the Watt home, a blonde woman, clearly in her cups, met us with a wide smile. In her manicured hand was a martini that she kept sipping as she gushed in a French accent about how glad she was to see us. We stepped carefully, one behind the next, into the full presence of a huge boa constrictor who had settled himself along the two walls of the pink and beige carpet of the spacious living room.

He raised his head. I was the only one who gasped, "Jesus! . . . What the hell is *that*?" No one else said a thing out loud as we held our breaths and filed politely down an adjoining staircase to an outdoor patio, fully catered with fruit and coffee and breakfast rolls. It was apparent to me that my trauma was showing: the fright of growing up on an Indian reservation where prairie rattlers are taken seriously. I sat at the patio table clutching my Georg Lukács text on theories of the novel, unable to eat a thing while what I thought of as the smiling and stretching and menacing reptile in the other room was not mentioned!

We discussed, under the guidance of Professor Watt, who was all intellectual business, the importance of Georg Lukács in understanding the significance of Marx and Kierkegaard. Both, we were told, were most deeply involved in the "life of the masses." I, honest to God, read *History and Class Consciousness* that summer.

Alienation in the twentieth century? Tell me about it!

The fields of philosophy and economics and sociology and literature show something about alienation in the twentieth century, and it all centers around Marxism in the works we read that summer in Palo Alto. Is there something ironic in the reality that Palo Alto is one of the richest places in America, and we were studying Marxism instead of capitalism?

That summer I read sentences like, "the function of theory is to understand the dialectical method." More practically, the function of theory is to eventually understand something about the world we live in, connected to historical experience. I hoped we would eventually get there.

On the weekends we drove to the beaches and read other stuff like Carl Sandburg's poetry. Karl Marx's favorite novelist, I learned, was Honoré de Balzac, but how that was relevant to our current situation was lost on me. I had discarded Balzac long ago because he seemed to be thoroughly a monarchist. The fact that he was a supporter of the old French aristocracy based in blood, though, interested me because the Sioux tiospaye (governing paradigm) is also based in blood.

I was still a smoker in those days, as were several others in the group. This was before the smoking ban found its way across the continent, even into the little bars I used to frequent in Spokane, Washington, with names like the Double Clutch Tavern and the Buck and Doe. There was even a place called Art Farkle's, and one could see many out-of-state Indian bureaucrats convening there from time to time.

In Watt's back yard, cigarette smoke wafted into the eucalyptus trees and the clear blue California sky. People drank pink champagne first, then started mixing the hard stuff, though it was only ten o'clock in the morning. We had a great time, but the reptile in the next room would not leave my thoughts. I saw him lifting his head, looking for me.

At three o'clock we went to our vehicles from the patio steps through the most beautifully cared-for garden of flowers I'd ever seen outside of a museum.

I was tempted to go back at the second invitation two weeks later, but the snake and the gushing drunk at the door kept me away.

Maybe because I possessed a mere undergraduate degree from the English and Journalism Department at South Dakota State College, Brookings, and maybe because I had studied literature at the University of Nebraska, Lincoln, with such important but isolated Plains literary stars as Lee Lemon and Hilda Raz, and even read the poetry of William Kloefkorn and Ted Kooser, I was at that time quite unaware of the intellectual ferment of the times. Reform was passing by such scholars of the Midwest as well as those of Victorian-age fiction, like Ian Watt, and moving toward the critical work of third-world notables like Edward Said, who would publish *Culture and Imperialism* years later (Knopf, 1993).

What I mean to say here is that all in all, I have had a very competent education but one that has been oddly inferior to third-world scholarship. Having had to grasp at straws during my professional career, I've always felt I've been stumbling around in academia like a hapless Magoo — blindly and narrowly missing catastrophes, happening upon a clear view of the busy highway of academe by mere chance.

In defense of myself, I was trying to run my life as a low-ranking academic and a divorcée with four children, and though I was reasonably successful at it, I was probably envying those who had the good luck to tell me they studied with *some notable* or had *read* at prestigious repositories around the globe. To read at Cambridge (or even the Newberry Library in Chicago) seemed to be the basis for discovery in some circles.

I came to understand how awful and humiliating it is to be the only one without a PhD sitting blindfolded in a summer seminar with people of a different class and academic rooting who wanted to take Rudyard Kipling's *Kim* seriously. We spent a lot of time on *A Passage to India*, perhaps because many of the ladies-in-waiting-in-tennis-shoes attending the seminar, who were among Watt's biggest fans, were on the verge of anthropology.

Professor Watt, I knew, had cowritten "The Consequences of Literacy" with the well-known British social anthropologist Jack Goody, who believed that since the Greeks had invented an alphabet and a writing system, they brought about urbanization, which, naturally, brought about civilization. Vine Deloria Jr., a versatile Native scholar who was going ballistic about the discipline of anthropology and its connection to colonialism at that time, always cautioned us to "keep an open mind."

I had read the Goody-Watt essay at some earlier point but had never thought of Watt as an anthropologist until I met him. Much can be said about the consequences of literacy. As one who speaks a Native language I cannot write, I find myself wondering about those consequences often. Linguistics, as a body of study, has been a mystery to me. But I have known learned Native people who could not write their own names.

One supposes that the rationale about civilization by scholars such as Goody is among the many reasons that the Maya and Aztec worlds, the Egyptian pyramids, Indian caves, and all manner of the discoveries of Arab antiquities have been deemed worthy of anthropological and literary investigation.

Incidentally, it's also why Hercule Poirot and Agatha Christie are, even today, masters of popular imperial fiction. I hate to admit it, but *Poirot* is always on my must-watch TV list Sunday evenings.

Such backgrounds in anthropology seemed to account for the interest of our seminarians in *A Passage to India*, even though we never mentioned the fact that we were characterizing mere stubbornness or foolishness on the part of the quaint East Indian characters, rather than uncovering the fury and hostility and blazing hatred toward imperialistic rule that was apparent to anyone who paid any attention at all to history. Even in the 1970s, Asia was becoming restless.

Much later, in 2001, after the 9/11 attack in New York crystallized the notion that the third world would no longer be silent about the imperial rule in its countries, the discussions we had engaged in during that seminar seemed an illogical betrayal of what we, as scholars, were spending time and treasure promoting. George W. Bush's reaction to 9/11 reminded me of what had gone unsaid in this academic setting and others like it, often called the Ivory Tower. Bush's unaccountable and plaintive "why do they hate us?" must ring in the ears of all of us even now who attended that humanities seminar and others like it. It certainly took away any interest American Indians, like myself, might have had in scholarship for scholarship's sake.

In spite of this kind of experience, we are still encouraged to send our best and brightest off to the Ivies to learn that saying nothing about imperial hegemony, which embodies the whole of the educational systems available, will get them an advanced degree, a home in Phoenix, and two or three cars in the garage. It has always been that way. Remember "a chicken in every pot"? That was our parents' window of opportunity, and the acceptance of it has meant that our shattered communities probably will not and perhaps cannot resist the pressures of the colonial system.

Thus, we make excuses. I attach much importance to the fact that I learned about writing in this humanities seminar I so cynically describe here and now. It must have been a catalyst for further work, I say, and that's a good thing.

We were asked by Professor Watt to write prolusions every week, sometimes more than one. For those of you who don't know what a prolusion is, it is a literary kind that can be taught in graduate schools as a preliminary exercise for further serious literary criticism. It is an essay that might be written, perhaps, by a presiding officer or chairman of the lower house of a convocation in an Anglican church. Or maybe not.

I kept telling myself, "this is England, folks, and I need to know this," as I pored over the irrelevant details of apathy expressed by Godbole, the surrealistic Hindu character in *A Passage to India*. I scribbled in my notes: "If Aziz is a Muslim nationalist, I am the man in the moon." But I quickly deleted it. And instead, I wrote that the trial of Aziz was probably the norm in the English court system, and it was Aziz's "timidity" and the trip to the Marabar Caves that revealed the complexity of the fictional situation. Isn't that what Forster wanted to envelop our attention as readers and critics?

I continued to long for the day when Professor Watt would talk more about the bridge on the river and how history becomes myth. I longed to be told by his eminence how this happens. What am I missing? Our professor mentioned it but once. And then just as an afterthought.

So much for applying for a humanities award–winning spot in a prestigious seminar, thinking you know what the professor wants to profess. So much for wanting to write something profound in comparison about the events that surround rivers, the Missouri River in particular, and the riverbed that once held the mythic histories now fed by converging tributaries, a place as old as the Kwai and the earth itself.

Such losses to imperialists are unbearable. For that moment, I knew I would have to leave that parchment bare, as I had chosen a distant image, and it would be years before I would take it up again. Ultimately, while probing some of the masterpieces of nineteenth-century fictionists, I learned more by accident along with my oppositional reading (undirected and unassigned) than I wanted to know about the versions of imperialism in the scholarly and imaginative writing of colonial nations.

This strange period of study, though, has probably connected itself to all of the interactive essays I've been writing in Indian studies for the last three decades. It has, perhaps unintentionally, led me to understand why Edward Said, years later, coined the phrase "contrapuntal reading," the point of which is, he says, that the reader "must take account of both processes, that of Imperialism and that of resistance to it which can be done by extending our reading of the texts to include what was once forcibly excluded.... In *L'Etranger*, for example, the whole previous history of France's colonialism and its destruction of the Algerian state, and the later emergence of an independent Algeria (which Camus opposed)" (*Culture and Imperialism*, 67). The counterpoint is what Said said was important in our reading of texts, and later third-world writers have taken it up: "Colonial and imperial realities are overlooked.... Few writers and critics ... discuss the relationship between culture and empire" (64).

At the time of the summer seminar, I had no reason to know these things because, very simply, I had not read enough. Thus, I just had to struggle in isolation with my discontent concerning the frighteningly useless discussions on *A Passage to India* and other Forsterian readings we were undertaking.

3

EVEN LATER, WHEN I was writing *Why I Can't Read Wallace Stegner*, I had no real understanding of what was forcibly excluded from Forster's work and, most significantly, from Stegner's oeuvre on Western America, nor could I examine my inchoate thoughts about it with any degree of sophistication. At that 1970 Palo Alto National Humanities seminar, third-world writings were still to be, it would seem in retrospect, unthought of and unshared in the cultural development of Western world scholarship.

My complaints in that early collection of essays, examining what I have found detestable about writers of the West like Stegner, seemed to some to be fairly petty and unfocused. Writing it got me invited to all kinds of events arranged by classically trained historians so they could argue with me about my inaccuracies. Readers either love that little book or hate it. It is still in print, now an ebook.

I will be forever grateful to a wonderfully astute editor at the University of Wisconsin Press named Rosalie Robertson, who, when she looked at the manuscript I had sent in with a title like "Exporting Scholarly Discourse in Fulfilling Native Destiny" or some such academic double-speak, immediately called me on the telephone and said in disbelief: "You're kidding—Liz, this is an interesting book, but frankly, no one would pick it up from a bookstore shelf with that awful title!"

She is the one who chose the title *Why I Can't Read Wallace Stegner*, and it turned out to be an appealing choice. It catches the eye because, surely, we know everybody reads Stegner.

Editors, I've found, matter! And good editors who not only know something about the publishing world but who care about highly particularized subject matters are rare indeed. *This*, I said to myself, *is an editor who doesn't mind telling you what you need to know.*

When I published those essays in 1996, it was my lame intention as an inadequate but determined Dakota Sioux writer to let people know that Lakotas, Dakotas, and Nakotas have *never* accepted American imperial/colonial government rule on treaty lands in spite of what people as diverse as Lewis and Clark, Thomas Sowell, Ralph K. Andrist, even Stanley Vestal, Mari Sandoz, George Catlin, and the Supreme Court have implied. They have never "vanished," as Stegner suggests, nor are they willing to give up their own stories.

I had always known that non-European (and by my extension, non-American) peoples did not accept with indifference the authority projected over them nor the general silence on which their presence in variously attenuated forms is predicated. This is what Edward Said had written in 1993 before I read *Culture and Imperialism*.

To be fair, current critics of all stripes are moving away from imperialistic and esoteric fantasies in novelistic work set in the eighteenth century or the nineteenth. Since my Palo Alto summer, I am encouraged that political criticism has started to take the place of sociological criticism in graduate schools across the country. And the social context of the boring eighteenth-century middle class has gone to television and the BBC. Nobody calls it essential literature around here anymore. Everybody is reading Noam Chomsky these days and the *Washington Post* and Salman Rushdie and the internet.

Nonetheless, many of my accidental discoveries proved useful. Dr. Watt and the scholars who interacted with me there were like the first Bedouin finders in the desert who brought the seven complete Dead Sea Scrolls to Bethlehem and started a great hullabaloo in archeology and literary studies and art. My fellow seminarians at Palo Alto did that for me.

I was sort of getting the idea that the significance of the Marabar Caves as metaphor could not be dismissed, yet could be easily attacked because we have to take it apart as though it is some kind of joke. Of course, I staggered onward. I could not fail.

4

BECAUSE OF ALL THIS, I later wrote a piece on Native American literatures using N. Scott Momaday's *House Made of Dawn* as an exemplar of how to bind American Indian aesthetics to the stream of consciousness technique in dialogue and fiction so aptly invented by previous fictionists, particularly the Bloomsbury Group in England. This was not profound. Indeed, it was barely adequate as lit-crit stuff. But it got me an invitation a couple of years later to the meeting focused on Native literatures by the Conference on College Composition and Communication journal people in New Orleans, where I was welcomed with open arms.

The truth is I had never been anywhere in the South, where the four Cs conference was being held. New Orleans was a real mystery. The first morning out of my hotel, I encountered a black Louisianan cab driver who spoke in tongues when I asked him where I could get a bus to the French Quarter. He gave elaborate directions, pointing up the street. I said, "mm-hmm, thanks," and stumbled toward where his long brown finger was pointing, though I didn't understand one word of his Cajun-accented English.

For me, the trek to famous New Orleans landmarks was more Mr. Magoo, something like a never-married woman trying to find a rich husband and looking for him in the file folders of *Forbes* magazine. That's a metaphor I've borrowed from some forgotten text, but doesn't it fit the occasion? When I got to the place where Tennessee Williams's streetcar named Desire was parked behind smoke-fogged glass windows, I knew I had found the promised land.

Here it was! The streetcar! It was an awesome sight with sounds to match, snuggled as it was between open doors on either side catering to strippers and Pete Fountain's jazz fans. I wandered about for several hours, past the joints with nude dancers and fabulous tobacco shops where I expected I might see the poet Victor Hernández Cruz, who once told me about the tobacconists of his home country, Puerto Rico, and showed those of us in a writer's workshop how to smoke the Cuba Rica cigars he sometimes carried.

I finally got back to the hotel, where I tried to tell the others of the sights and the sounds and the well-rehearsed tour guide who knew everything there was to know of Williams, calling him Tennessee as though she knew him. My hotel mates seemed totally uninterested, none of them having read Williams or any other modern novels, nor anything except BIA pamphlets and management reports since they had graduated from college. They were a bunch of Indian bureaucrats and program managers in New Orleans to expose the gentry of academe to American Indians from the Plains.

A couple of them were directors of federal programs from North Dakota and South Dakota. They delivered boring reports of their efforts at curriculum development, while Pat Locke, who claimed Hunkpapa ancestors, just in from California, was there to perform the Lord's Prayer in sign language. She was not a Lakota nor Dakota speaker and was in the process of moving back to the reservation with her children. Later, she told my friends at home how impressed she was that I had actually delivered a stunningly well-prepared academic paper on literary criticism and aesthetics.

Pat was the cosmopolitan among us and took pride in arranging an evening of dining out at a soul food restaurant located quite near where the Saints games were being played at that time. I think that arena has since been pulled down and replaced. We all dressed to the nines and gathered at the rotunda to gulp down several, yes, mint juleps at the bar before piling into yellow and black taxi cabs for an incredible charge toward downtown New Orleans.

The feast before us included fried catfish, sea food gumbo, skillet cornbread, corn pudding, grits, chitlins and maw, black-eyed peas, dirty rice, collard greens with meat, and meeting house potato salad. We drank some more, laughed, and counted ourselves among the lucky reservation Indians to be living the good life.

When I think about this period in my life I do not get nostalgic for it; indeed, I am ashamed and astounded at the lack of dedication we showed at some of these gatherings. Many people I knew then who weren't with us on our jet encounters were living desperate lives with no jobs and no hope of getting an education. They lived as my father did, in a two-room house built by the U.S. government in 1920 with no running water, no curtains, and the prairie wind blowing hot and dry across the living room space toward the shining river.

I have become sure years later that the races in America should not live together, and that's okay. I could never tell these people in New Orleans, black or white, who we really were, that my father believed the unktechies lived in the water he could see from the window of his house and that the turtle was a holy being that at one time had long legs and could run very fast, that he carried around his neck bits of turtle shells as well as his umbilical cord in a pouch made for him by his grandmother not quite a hundred years ago that he called a chekpa.

Perhaps, I'm thinking, we should not even go as tourists to the center of each others' lives. Two opposing nationalisms met that night: Native ethnocentrism and Africanism. There were no whites there, no third parties, and we were like strangers in a strange land. We were not nearly as adept as black people at going it alone, yet that is what we wanted more than anything—to go it alone. We knew we were the colonized people but not slaves, and we thought that made all the difference.

Maybe not. It was W. E. B. Du Bois, after all, a black intellectual, who propounded in America of all places, as early as 1897, the idea that black men would have to be freed from oppression by going it alone. But of course he, unlike his Indian counterpart, did not possess land and treaties and gold and water and the trees that white men coveted and killed for. In his case, there was no need for negotiations to avoid theft and genocide. I thought then and I still do that there is something inevitable about our lives, yet there is nothing destructive about them, only outspoken claims to our uniqueness and casual connections.

When it was time to go, Pat went to the phone book in the foyer of the restaurant and called up seven taxi cab companies — each of which was "not available" — all the while noticing the handsome grinning face of the bartender polishing his glassware. She finally turned and, despairingly, flopped down on a stool and was stunned to hear him say quietly, "Ma'am, taxis don't come to this part of town after ten o'clock."

He raised his eyebrows as she raced back to our table, which by now looked like a crime scene, most of us bleary-eyed from food and drink. She nearly shouted, "Hey, people, taxis don't come here after ten o'clock," to the entire room of diners. We stared at her, and the room got incredibly quiet. Everyone in the restaurant was looking at us. As we looked back, we wondered, *Where are we? What should we do?* We could envision a long walk to our hotel through hostile territory, and we started looking in our purses and pockets for the address of the place we'd spent the previous nights.

At that point, a suave black gentleman dressed in elegant white-tie attire came to our table and said, "Don't worry, folks. . . . Don't worry."

"It's okay, ma'am," he said to Pat, who was by now in full swing of a crying jag caused as much from drink as the stress of the last few moments. He led us to the side entrance of a spacious, brightly lit garage where several Mercedes and Cadillacs were parked and asked, "What's the address?" He gathered up two more drivers and, laughing all the way like they were in on some massive joke, they sped us to our hotel.

By this time, we were fairly sober and, for sure, not laughing.

We gathered for a moment in my room on the twelfth floor, and while the director of Indian studies at the University of North Dakota rescued a bottle of scotch from his jacket pocket and started mixing more drinks, I was still asking, "Where the hell are we?"

Pat kicked off her red cowboy boots and passed out from exhaustion on my double bed, her luxurious black hair with a white streak down one side, so carefully brushed for most of the evening, now a mass of tangles.

I was mad at the whole lot of us.

"Hey," I said to Frank, "I don't let people crash in my place. . . . Take your drinks and her"—I pointed at Pat—"*out* of here!" I opened the door and watched him gather her up, fling her arms over his shoulders, and head for the elevator. The others straggled after them. I don't remember what happened to the red cowboy boots, but someone must have retrieved them because later that summer when I saw her at Crow Fair in Montana, she was wearing them.

There was a period of time when we so-called academics and intellectuals of the Indian world traveled in smart circles and were called, derisively by others who knew what the stakes were, "the jet set." What we were doing or what we thought we were doing, spreading the gospel, was probably of dubious value. There was money and funding sources of all kinds for education during that brief time, so today I know many people who hold several academic degrees, debt free of school loans. Many professionals today in the Indian world came from dire poverty and never had to pay their own way because of the availability of scholarships. They, in fact, could not have achieved higher education without the federal mandate.

There was at that stunning moment the national effort to make scholarship money available to poverty enclaves called reservations in order to get Native peoples into the academic mainstream. That period was called the affirmative action period in our national lexicon, and it brought a whole generation of qualified Indian students into professional fields like law and economics and business and management, as well as the academic disciplines. The educational landscape is quite different for today's Native students who are, by and large, in debt up to their ears with school loans or dropped out entirely because of lack of money.

Pat, one of those lucky recipients of scholarship monies, was a smart, respected executive type who in 1991 was awarded a MacArthur Foundation grant. It was one of those awards called a genius grant. She did a lot of work in education and Dr. Dean Chavers, the founder of a Native American scholarship fund, considered her an important modern American Indian leader and said so in one of his many books. Pat died in Arizona in 2001 at seventy-three years of age and was among the prominent Indians who professed the Bahá'í Faith, so she was buried there within a day of her passing. I later went to an honoring ceremony for her in Rapid City, South Dakota, and was given a beautiful blanket, which I keep among my treasures.

Our restaurant table of a dozen or so Indians was the only table of non–African Americans in the room, so we created quite a stir. It was an experience that made me sure I would not write about people, just ideas. "Where do Indians fit in?" was my ubiquitous question. I knew we didn't. Since those halcyon days, Indians were to gather from all over the country to form protest movements called Red Power and the American Indian Movement. Some said we modeled it after the Black Power Movement. I'm sure that is not the case, since our writers and poets were more likely to use the term *ancestors* than *motherfuckers*.

That's changed now. We, too, because the protest movements of the time were flourishing, would change our vocabulary and become among the rowdy, most reviled people in our northern and prairie states, living separately, just as African Americans lived separate lives in their region. Racist policies by bad governments all over the world had to be fought, though, and I guess the impetus to be yourself is the same everywhere. I look back now in some kind of brief disappointment for our momentary abandon, knowing even then these were crucial times but being unwilling to pay the price.

5

DURING THIS TIME I continued my writing. Moving my family about as I pursued advancement was a huge source of anxiety and eventual regret, and as I enrolled at the University of Nebraska in Lincoln for a while to work on my PhD, we all reoriented ourselves to new situations.

I had been awarded a leave of absence from my teaching position at Eastern, so I was on half pay. While at Nebraska, I completed the course work and proposed a dissertation topic that was accepted by a committee of people I never met and never knew. I wrote several long, long prolusions and did my research, but instead of finishing the dissertation, I started writing and publishing books, much to my dismay in retrospect. I regret not possessing a PhD not only because it is an entrance to further study and financial assistance but because it was my mother's earliest admonition that finishing what you start is a way to success.

It is a truism that everyone in the English department at UNL had fallen under the spell of Willa Cather ever since and probably before *My Antonia*, and though I was unable to get into the classics class taught in her name, I went dutifully in quest of Willa Cather like everyone else. I read all of her works while there, even though the prosaic questions her fiction asked did not fit into my inchoate school of contemporary criticism at the time, that is, the attachment for what might have been called the commonplace values. This was when there was an argument about the function of spirituality in

American life vis-à-vis Ernest Hemingway and other disenchanted American exiles.

For the first time I began to understand the farmers in Cather's home stronghold, Nebraska (and probably South Dakota too), and their relentlessly positive treatment of European colonization. They have always been more interested, perhaps, in the orderly life than in understanding the reasons for the Indian raids that their ancestors tolerated. Thus colonization, which was the source of the raids and the stealing of treaty justice, was never considered a crime. It was simply a way to struggle a new and orderly life in a new land.

My resentment toward all of this grew, but the truth is I couldn't bear the boredom of working on a dissertation and quickly went back to teaching and writing what I wanted to write! In order to achieve a doctorate, I've been told, you have to really, really *want* it. What I have always really wanted is to write. Please notice I didn't say I wanted to be a writer or to get published. I have very simply wanted to experiment with language and find out more clearly what I really think.

Without an agent and, frankly, with only a narrow reading audience, I have struggled to publish eleven books with university presses, remaining ABD. I spend almost as much time trying to engage publishers as I spend writing. Many of my books have fallen quickly into obscurity, and many of them are said by critics to engender anger and hatred in readers who do not agree with my sentiments. When I first started publishing books, major historians who shall remain nameless were not impressed because my view of America's hypocrisy was too left-wing for "scholarly" texts.

One of those historians even said to my editor Liz Dulany at a University of Illinois Press convention, "Why are you publishing Cook-Lynn? . . . She surely does *not* deserve a university press!"

An old conservative-minded contention goes something like this: Indian writers are on the margin and really have little to offer in terms of unbiased scholarship. I am forever grateful to Dulany, who stood by my work in heroic ways. Even when I stopped talking to the copyeditor assigned to work with me on *The Politics of Hallowed Ground: Wounded Knee and the Struggle for Indian Sovereignty* (University of Illinois Press, 1999), Dulany managed to keep us on the right track.

One time, when the copyeditor argued with a statement I made about the political climate surrounding Sitting Bull's assassination and asked for changes, I insisted that my phrase not be modified. I even confronted the copyeditor, saying, "the only function of a copyeditor is to make sure that if the car is blue on page 12, it is still blue on page 98!"

"Well, now, Cook-Lynn," said Dulany in her reasonable way, "that is probably an exaggeration, don't you think?" I didn't say it out loud, but I thought: *Well, if that copyeditor wants to write a book, tell her to go ahead. This one is mine.*

Even my cowriter, Mario Gonzalez, and I had our nerves frayed. I think he went away saying, "Hey, don't ever write a book with a poet," and I said, "Don't ever write a book with a lawyer." Dulany was a saint through it all. And all of us ended up knowing that this book would contribute mightily to the emerging discipline of tribal literatures. Even today, Gonzalez calls it sui generis. It contains an invaluable section of appendixes for those researchers interested in the subject matter.

I went about doing some belated graduate work. A search for a theory of aesthetics seemed to be the endless focus at Nebraska. I even read *Zen and the Art of Motorcycle Maintenance* by Robert M. Pirsig as a last-ditch effort. It wasn't particularly stimulating because what Zen tells us, I guess, is what we all know: that quality in aesthetics must always be kept undefined, as the receiver of language and thought always has to pass this crest himself.

I'm sure I found this mildly interesting but not particularly profound because as writers we've always known we may never be able to define in absolutes what we want to say. Knowing more languages than English, I would think, might help in this search, because it is a fact that I can say some things in the Dakota Sioux language that I cannot say in English, which means that producing rich prose in English is not all there is to it. My study of other languages is sadly neglected.

English dialectic is, after all, the form that takes you toward logical conclusion, and isn't it the place where Aristotle started? In what language? Greek? The barriers to true aesthetic sensitivity remain unclear in my mind, and I am still afraid of my own inadequacy. The study of many languages is almost vital in literary critical studies.

At that time at Nebraska, we were reading a lot in linguistics theory, which is what *Motorcycle Maintenance* is all about. I was reading N. Scott Momaday too. I am his greatest fan and have decided that years from now we will still be standing at the altar waiting to hear what he has to say about aesthetics and what is sacred and what is profane. That's just the way it was then and continues to be.

All I really got out of what Pirsig was saying was that in maintaining his motorcycle he was dealing with concepts, not parts. Really? I don't see how dealing with linguistics conceptually is different from dealing with it grammatically, yet our professor seemed to believe it was different. In addition to that made-up dilemma, we spent a lot of time in linguistics talking about the question of where language comes from.

One of our charming but mocking colleagues reminded us in one of our strange class discussions that birds probably do have some kind of language, and we agreed, but he insisted that they probably sing just for fun. Not to communicate. Not to survive. They cannot lie, and they have no ability to create new things, he pointed out.

On the contrary, I argued, they sing to communicate just as everyone else does. Have you ever seen a meadowlark who makes her nest on the ground fake a broken wing to lead varmints away from her young? She often sings throughout the ordeal, which, I'm sure, cannot be thought of as "fun." All of this argument about singing for fun was to support the uniqueness of humans, I was thinking. Even the African American poet Maya Angelou, in one of the stunning collections of her poems I read later, confuses the matter when she says, "A bird doesn't sing because it has an answer, it sings because it has a song!"

When I tried to tell my colleagues that I heard the meadowlark in Washington State sing a different song from the ones I heard her sing out on the Crow Creek and proposed that there was a message in that, it seemed just like a simple-minded story, not profundity, not theory. At the time, we could not get past the idea that birds just sing for fun, as the uninventive guy kept insisting. After listening to my colleagues take this man seriously, I began to fear that one of the decisive factors in obtaining a PhD was to lead the charge in stupidity. If you can bully your way throughout an academic discussion without causing a fractious relationship with your colleagues, your point will be made. I went away thinking of language as a survival mechanism and have continued to believe that birds want to survive too.

Hostility toward Chomsky and others of his ilk was profound in some of the classes I took at the University of Nebraska in those days! And when we couldn't answer the question of whether thought could exist without language, we were simply told to "go read chapter 9." There seemed to be no clear answers.

In the process of thinking about language as survival, I read *The Arrowmaker* by N. Scott Momaday. (I've never read much anthropology nor Franz Boas, so I could be on the wrong track.) When we ask ourselves if any part of the story could legitimately be omitted, we illustrate the ongoingness, the interrelatedness, the parameters, and the attachments in the process of language. Could the owl's sound (*who-ooo-ooo*) have been omitted? No. If it had been omitted, the arrowmaker, the would-be scout, could not have dropped his arrow and seen the face in the tipi opening, thus making prediction impossible.

"The sound startled him," we are told, and he shot his arrow straight up through the face looking down at him. It is survival, after all, that is the crux of the issue in the illustrative story about the young scout. Always before, in thinking about the story, I focused on the fact that the scout asks in Kiowa who is out there. When there is no answer, he shoots his arrow because if you don't know the Kiowa language, you are obviously an intruder. It's a little like Lakota and Dakota language speakers. We often think, *if you don't know our language, you might be an enemy, even called to-ka.* Slightly ethnocentric, perhaps. The sound of the owl, though, makes it possible for us to say it is not just words that we can translate. It is sound too.

Sound, then, may be considered the initiator of language. We can, of course, suggest that language exists without this kind of unconscious initiator in the process of survival, but we cannot say that language does not exist for the purpose of survival.

That the young scout is alive and his enemy dead is what makes this story a powerful illustration of how and why we acquire language and how and why we cannot survive without this knowledge. Whether the bird, just singing for fun, is less interested in survival than humans are is doubtful. Whether the question posed in Kiowa words by the arrowmaker is all that is necessary is also doubtful.

At about this time, I was trying to think this through, so I wrote down what an old flute player from home who reminded me of that fictional arrowmaker once told me:

This Story
I've just told you when I played the song,
the flute player said
when the long and excessive
sounds echoed its unbearable memory
neither of us can put into words. . . . it is very sad. . . .
It is about a woman who is leaving and she turns and
    waves her shawl, and
he thinks he may not see her again, but I don't have to tell
    you the story in
words, I can just tell it with the sounds of the flute. Words
    can be a part of
it, the flute player said, but they aren't necessary.

I still keep on my desk the wooden flute carved by that old man who told me this. He gave it to me as a gift, and I treasure it even though I note that he apologized at the same time because, "you know, old men are not supposed to play these songs. . . . They are love songs. Only young men should play them." Maybe that's why he gave me the beautiful flute, because he was no longer young and neither was I.

Other than episodes like meeting up with this Winnebago flute player, my Nebraska days were a study in the demolition of expectations. Two days after registration time in Nebraska, my daughters and I had driven from the Crow Creek into the city of Lincoln during a rain storm. It rained for nearly two weeks, which meant that the sun didn't shine and, in turn, that I didn't know directions in that town for several weeks.

The three girls went to three different schools, and there seemed to be no school buses nor city buses in our area, making it quite difficult for me to find our way around and get them to their appointed schools (elementary, junior high, and high school) on time.

I was late registering for my own classes, so when I tried to get into Bernice Slote's Writers of the Plains seminar, I was told that there were already twenty registrants. When I timidly asked if I could be the twenty-first, Professor Slote said with some indignity, "Surely you must know that a seminar can't be taught with twenty-*one* people in it."

I believe that misconceptions play a huge role in shaping one's place in the world, so when I drove through the city streets and mistakenly thought that west was south and east was south and that a seminar could surely be taught with twenty-*one* in it just as well as with twenty, the situation seemed eerily like so many others I encountered.

Doubts about how one can be reduced to a clear reminder of one's massive flaws felt a little bit like the fiscal doubts that were also overwhelming me. My application for a Ford fellowship had been denied, and I had to borrow seven hundred dollars from my mother. Otherwise, my kids and I eked out an existence on an assistant professor's half salary. We didn't last long, and I had to give it up before achieving my doctorate.

Years later, when I was an associate professor and was invited by the Ford fellowship committee to be a reader, scholar, and consultant for others who were applying for the grant, I damn near turned them down just to satisfy my revenge. I thought, *if I can't get an award as an applicant, why am I reading as a consultant the proposals of others who can?* What stopped me was that to be a reader and consultant for the Ford fellowship would *look good on my vita.* Not as good as actually being a recipient, but good. Being ABD, I was still on the lower end of the totem pole and could hardly afford to be snotty about it. I've not applied for anything major since.

We ate a lot of eggs that semester in Lincoln, fried, scrambled, omeletized, boiled. Our apartment was on the second floor, just above a young couple with an infant. The baby was silent as a mouse, but the parents argued, cried, hollered, screamed, and threatened each other throughout the night, throwing things and slamming doors, sometimes all night, after which the young father would emerge from their door into the sunshine, dressed neatly, showered, and shaved, hopping in his Chevy and waving goodbye to his lovely wife, who was seen strolling the baby around the quad for a morning break.

The guy was obviously, to me anyway, a wife abuser, and she was a weeper who believed that when the sun came up, all was well. I was thinking to myself, *been there, done that,* but my daughters were fascinated and crowded around the grate in our hallway floor for hours every night to hear the show, gasp, and whisper. We could not afford a television, so we were willing to make considerable sacrifices.

I had previously made arrangements to read a scholarly paper at the November MLA meeting in Denver, Colorado, and my department had made travel arrangements, so my eldest daughter (with the others in tow) drove me to the Lincoln airport, and I flew off for three days on a crowded Frontier flight, leaving them to their own devices in a town where they now knew the bus routes but not one adult soul!

I felt like Mayzie the lazy bird, who flew off to Miami in the children's story we had read together. What kind of mother leaves her young daughters alone in a town we had lived in for little more than one month, where we knew no one, and where there was no one to help them in a crisis? "This is my telephone number in Denver," I assured them.

"Well, we have the car, so don't worry," my sixteen-year-old daughter replied, not recognizing the images of horror any parent hearing those words from her teenager might be conjuring up.

The youngest, always practical but ready, too, for a getaway, piped up, looking at the dials, "and a tank of gas."

It seems worth noting here that this was not an unusual circumstance for these daughters as I pursued my so-called career. Many years later, we could laugh about it as I often exclaimed to my colleagues with a strange mixture of pride and sheepishness, "I raised my children by telephone."

They became experts at believing in the notion that they were independent beings and that their mother would let them run their own lives. They've come down from that high, but all in all they've done an admirable job raising themselves and each other and me. I am forever grateful to them. My son by this time refused to have much to do with us (a mother and three younger sisters?), so he stayed in Cheney, Washington, with his good friends. He married early and has gone about his life.

I have always thought, though, that since I had kept a roof over his head, he owed me things like information, explanations, telephone calls, fidelity, mundane little aspects of his life, but, he, too, has become an independent soul who belongs to no one. That seems to be a trait of this little family I've claimed.

After our year-long Nebraska fling, we went back to Cheney, Washington, where I quickly won tenure and an associate relationship with my colleagues at EWU. We stayed there for twenty years.

6

WHEN MY ELDEST DAUGHTER was ready for high school, she tried the public school in Cheney but quickly found it wasn't to her liking and went off to the Institute of American Indian Arts in Santa Fe, New Mexico. It was the hardest time of my life except when my second daughter became an exchange student and flew off to Bogotá, Colombia, at seventeen. She was in Medellín a whole academic year and two summers. This was during the Pablo Escobar days, and the mail was agonizingly slow and phones didn't work, so there was much to worry about.

Marnie, my youngest, hung in there with me in Cheney, Washington, finally getting to ride in the front seat of our car when we drove anywhere, saying, "This is great! I always wanted to be an only child." Out of the shadows of her older siblings, she did well, found her creative muse, and took up writing and music and broadcasting. During that time of the eighties and ever since, I suppose, I ignored much of what was going on with my unfolding family, and as I look back on it now, they were pretty much on their own. Regret is often the name of this game.

I wanted to write essays for such places as the *New York Review of Books* and *The Nation* and *Vanity Fair*, so I went to a couple of workshops where they told you, "If you write something really good, you will get published." Maybe so, but not by the *New York Review of Books* nor *The Nation* nor *Vanity Fair*. Not if you are writing about Indians who are supposed to be vanished or about what an awful, racist, and self-interested place the American heartland really is! That is not considered good by most American publishing organs that appeal to the American mainstream, who want to hear about the little house out there in the middle of nowhere or Indian shamans. If you write about Indians, please write about praying to the Great Spirit or how drunk we all are since Lewis and Clark came . . . not about genocide, invasion, racist law, and the hideously righteous and narrow-minded Christians who came and built schools all over the West to capture the young.

Even a popular political writer like Paul Krugman does not go back far enough to get it. His *The Great Unraveling*, which I read not too long ago and consider one of the good analytical books of our time, well researched and cleverly written, suggests that America's goodness can be assessed and acclaimed if we don't talk about who was here first, the Indians, the invasion of the occupied West, the death of First Nations.

He's like a lot of important writers in today's milieu, where the doctrinal hatred of Indians in America has always been a reality to be avoided. To fail to acknowledge this important past gives us the substance for much of today's woes, but to speak of it in a substantial way is still not what most American writers, even political ones, thrive on. Even Melville found that out more than a hundred years ago.

When I happened upon the work of Richard Drinnon and his monumental research and history of America called *Facing West: The Metaphysics of Indian-Hating and Empire-Building*, I knew he was more than a political polemicist like a lot of the so-called "new" historians I'd been reading. Drinnon really did understand the hatred that spawned the racism that began America, even though, I think, he blames aggressive capitalism, that empirical impulse, a bit too much. The Drinnon book published by the University of Minnesota Press is one of the most comprehensive and most readable of Western histories about a nation's hatred of its indigenous peoples. There are few books like this one, and it should be assigned for every inquisitive scholar.

The reason I'm unhappy with the Drinnon emphasis on capitalism is not because it is false but because I think the *hate referenced in the title* is not given its due. Hate is not just a sub-emotion with causes and rationale and reason that can be counted on, a thing to be rid of when we grow up or come to our senses. I think hate is, rather, as legitimate a human emotion as love, which some say is the *primary* human need. Don't you think that is what Shakespeare is saying about Iago's hatred of Othello? That to hate is to be human? That it is a human need? Iago is not driven by jealousy or money or status. He is just one of those humans who has the human need to hate, and he seeks a victim.

Hate is as primary an emotion as any I can think of, not a sub-emotion or the going-awry of the human impulse. As I've aged, I have decided that hate is as primal a need of human beings as any other. It is only cultural behavior and language that eliminates it in a practiced and sustained effort.

Americans, Drinnon tells us, are capable of deep-seated hatred through refusing to accept Native Americans as persons, notions reinforced by parchment declarations and sculptors. These brilliant men and artists all, just like Iago, could not help themselves, and they know no remorse. They must be chastised through law, perhaps, which has to be a societal matter.

If these doings of civilized persons are not based in simple and profound hatred of white against Indian or settler against indigene, how else can we account for the continued spewing of oppression in parchment, stone, canvas, legend, and print available in today's marketplaces and repositories and halls of justice?

The Long Death by Ralph K. Andrist, for example, is not scholarship nor history, though it's accepted as such by classical historians in western regions. Instead, it is a striking example of putting on paper a narrative to satisfy hatred's need for the destruction of a people, much like hate's need to destroy love in the Othello/Desdemona story. There are entire libraries made up of this kind of scholarship based on historical hatred by colonists of indigenists.

What hate does is destroy, according to Shakespeare. Sadly, it is essential to the ups and downs of the human spirit and it continues to live with us . . . in our midst and alongside us as humans. Like death and taxes, hate will not only always be with us, as they say, but more realistically, it will continue to be a basic human trait. Many tribal societies have believed that evil exists alongside humans, and that's why they have ceremonies and rituals, to control evil, because it never goes away, is never defeated.

To talk of America's beginnings is not to say that American Indians are not also capable of deep-seated hatred. Indians are human too. I grew up with a grandmother who hated whites. She rarely spoke English and, oddly, in some kind of strange contradiction that she was often reminded of by her Ihanktowan husband (who refused to accompany her), walked two miles every Sunday to attend service at a Presbyterian church near the Crow Creek, where Christianity and assimilation was preached and the sermon rendered in her Dakota language. She tried valiantly to be a Presbyterian. Another odd contradiction.

Her relatives from Sisseton, people related to Solomon Two Stars, often gave the sermons. No one mentioned, nor did I hear the story until I was an adult, that Two Stars, an avowed Christian in 1862, had shot his teenaged son to death when the young man tried to ride out of the compound to join Little Crow's war against the whites in Minnesota that fateful summer. It was a war of survival, and the young man knew it. It was a war led by Little Crow's people, who detested what the thieving Christians among them were doing.

This grandmother of mine learned to hate whites out of that war that was, one supposes, a learned hatred and certainly based in many contradictions. It may have been something more primal in her. She always referred to the invaders as "fat takers," which was a reference to their greed in taking over Dakota lands.

Her other aversions to whites, however, seem to me in retrospect to be based in something more inexplicable. She avoided her white neighbors, many of them of German ancestry, because of their strong underarm odor and what she considered their excessive body hair. She spoke of that trait in uncomplimentary terms, often pondering why they had hair all over their bodies but not on their heads.

Hair was a sacred thing to her and she wore hers, even when it turned snow white, very long, even reaching to the floor. She wound it up and covered it with a black scarf. When her sons were sent off to the military boarding school by the U.S. government where their hair was cut off, she mourned the cutting of their hair almost as much as she mourned their absence.

Her sons lived to old age. One of them, my father, died in the Saint Mary's Hospital (unlike many of my relatives who died at home), and we kept watch on his disintegration, which seems in retrospect to have been fairly passive. Her only daughter died of tuberculosis in the early forties, and I can still hear the keening songs the old woman and her Santee relatives sang at the four-day wake held in a one-room shack behind the Grace Mission church grounds at Crow Creek. The daughter's sons, my cousins, lived with us from then on. That funeral ceremonial remains vivid because it was the last time I heard those sad mourning songs, and when I try to sing them, it is at that moment that I understand the hopelessness of calling back what we have lost to modernity.

Death, it seemed to me then, was a constant companion in that community, and it was taken as a wonder by those who had known each other all their lives. A paradox but at the same time an inevitability. These were not people who were moving about the country, to Texas or Alaska or Nashville or Seattle. No fresh starts for these folks. They had a community, and they had ancestral lands and were caretakers of it. This sense of place and the responsibility to it has been the center of strength and the future for so many in the past.

I wonder if its loss accounts for the reality that the suicide rate of our young people is higher than that of most other groups. Earlier this year, someone who was close to me but at the same time rather distant could not wait for the end that comes with old age; instead, he hanged himself in his other grandmother's backyard. He was seventeen years old. He was so young, undirected, undereducated, and, for me, another mysterious example of the workings of the human soul, death, and hatred. He hated his life, apparently, and seemed to be without the satisfying community of the past.

He was what is often called in today's lexicon the post-adolescent, pre-adult, in the not-quite-decided life stage that we often find excuses for. Long after the grief and dust have settled, I have to remind myself that suicide is an angry and selfish and hateful act, very unlike the death of my grandmother and her kin, to whom suicide was virtually unknown. I don't know what it has to do with hatred. Or self-hatred. Or hatred of life. No matter what comprehensive studies are done about young Indian suicide, the truth of *we'll never know*, is what is so unacceptable. All the pages of words will never make those, even those we think we know well, ever fully knowable. What secrets did this young man take with him? We will *never* know. That's what haunts us. I've known only two youthful suicides over the years, but being a grandmother makes such events particularly wrenching. I am confident that the loss of a sense of place is a cause.

A month before this young man killed himself, he and the family had taken me (as a traditional "old woman" dancer, a part of what I cynically consider the "golden-age" dancer category of the modern wacipi) to a communal dance at a nearby college, where my youngest grandchild wore her jingle dress for the first time. We danced together, and we were not thinking of death or hatred, only the future. The songs were familiar and place oriented.

At the dance, this young man held my shawl and spoke of how "neat" it was to be there, and he thanked all of us for inviting him even though he was neither dancer nor singer. I still see him, his heavy black hair shining above a pair of dark glasses that may have hidden his real thoughts, watching the ceremony, munching fries, going out for a smoke, and laughing together with us and the young people he knew.

If suicide is an angry and selfish and hateful act, why can't I blame him? Why am I still asking what I might have done? Why are his mother and his other grandmother inconsolable? His mother has still not gone back to the house where she raised him.

Why am I still asking why I wasn't more helpful, even though he was one of those people of that generation I've been known to complain about, who have been taking so long to grow up? I didn't know him well in life, so why am I still asking to know something more about him in that critical moment of his death when he just said "to hell with it"?

Was he despondent? (I don't know.) Was he desperate? (I don't know.) Was he angry? (I don't know.) Did he hate us, or himself? (I don't know.) Why didn't I . . . we . . . know the extent of his upheavals and vulnerabilities? To console myself, I wrote this poem.

Suicide

I grew one tomato that summer in a pot
on the cedar deck of that old house
a measure of my willingness to fail or not
I harvested it just as I returned
from the hall where I saw him laid out
in a shroud of silken maroon.
A single fruit among the dried yellow buds
now sits on my kitchen table among
dishes he dried just last morning
"That's a puny tomato," he said smiling.
"Your crop's gone bad, k unchida."
We can offer no explanation
for what has been happening to the disappeared ones

those we expected to bloom, those we thought
could make it from flower to fruit. We look for reasons:
maybe like some others
we watered too much or not enough
or otherwise poisoned the crops with too much salt
I pick up the tomato
like a waterlogged stone, it's in my hands
to know,
or say,
but drought remains
a possibility
what ran underground
we'll never know.

Because I often don't know what else to do with the events of my life that unravel every now and then, I have continued to think that writing can be among the solutions to such witnessing. In this poem, family activity is a poignant reminder of what we owe.

If we don't think that writing and education are among the answers to chaos, we really should try to recognize that there are few alternatives. What we tell the children of the future has always been a fundamental reason for my teaching and writing, and those children must be convinced that there are alternatives in their lives that matter.

7

YEARS AGO, WHEN I was just learning to be a new grandmother in the spring of 1985, the first issue of the Indian studies journal called the *Wicazo Ša Review* ("Red Pencil Review") was published from my office at Eastern Washington University. My dual teaching appointment in English and Indian studies was the hub of my world in those days, and starting a magazine was a relief from teaching assignments.

It seemed like a way to record some history in the academic setting that had become my life, even as my family life was getting more complicated. And it seemed, too, to be a lifeline thrown out into an indifferent sea of paper trails leading nowhere. I think of it now as an attempt to avoid my own suicide. If that seems a bit dramatic, it is. It was not suicide I was trying to avoid. It was boredom, ennui, weariness, harping on the same string of nouns and verbs, dangling participles, the Allotment Act, Indian Wars, and other academic instincts. The tedium of the pre-test, post-test world called undergraduate studies was becoming a stupid, dull, *crambe repetita*. Being a grandmother helps one through dismal times.

What was happening in Indian studies even in those early years was that the subject matter was becoming less distinguishable from other disciplines (anthropology, for one) that were like combat zones rather than spaces of learning. I wanted to proceed toward survival mechanisms.

Since much of what was going on in curricular development at that time emerged from activist English departments, a lot of literature, poetry, and creative writing by Indians made up the pages of this journal in its early stages. In the beginning, many mistakenly thought it was a literary journal rather than an Indian studies publication, probably a direct response to the heavy-handed influence of humanities and arts departments and scholars.

Yet political and historical documents were published and eventually became the major subject matter of the publication. A wonderfully talented writer, Dr. Roxanne Dunbar-Ortiz, who was at that time an associate professor in American Indian studies in the Department of Ethnic Studies at California State University, Hayward, let us reprint her article "Developing Indian Professionals" from the Center for Equal Education, Amherst, Massachusetts. She also lent her scholarly credentials by agreeing to be one of the associate editors for *Wicazo Śa*. Later, when she mistakenly thought she could use the journal's name and her name to solicit funds for some activist work in South America, she was asked to step down. At that point we hadn't wanted to get into the Contra-Sandinista conflict in South America, which may have been a mistake on our part.

We published in the first issue a report by Ward Churchill, who was already a published writer and a delegate to the International Indian Treaty Council. His timely article was entitled "The Situation of Indigenous Populations in the United States: A Contemporary Perspective." Many years later he was chastised by the University of Colorado and fired because of what they called inadequate research for his academic opinions expressed in his books.

Even though there was no restriction in the *Wicazo Śa* guidelines that contributors had to be Natives, our emphasis on publishing the works of Native scholars gave the impression of that requirement. Thus, it wouldn't be long before these two scholars, Dunbar-Ortiz and Churchill, would be in a messy academic mud-fight over the question of who was an Indian and who was not, how much Indian he or she was, and who could prove it by various and sundry evidence, none of which included enrolled citizenship and birth papers from a federally recognized tribal nation.

M. A. Jaimes, Churchill's associate, rendered a favorable review of his book on economics and *Wicazo Ṡa* editors, in retrospect probably conned into believing it was her work when more likely it was his, published it.

The journal proved to be as eclectic as its editors and contributors, yet its focus was always an Indian studies disciplinary approach. Those who appeared in the volume 1, number 1 issue were the poets Simon Ortiz, Joy Harjo, William Willard, Tom Holm, William Oandasan, Maurice Kenny, and a poet named Asa Primeaux Sr.

My profile on a peyote singer I knew, Asa Primeaux Sr. from the Yankton Sioux Tribe, may have seemed a little out of place since his work was truly grassroots rather than academic. His songs were tribal songs, and I had heard my Uncle Ted, a resident of Greenwood, South Dakota, sing them at the secretive Native American Church meetings a long time ago. Asa made tapes available to the academic community, and it was the position of the editors at *Wicazo Ṡa Review* that oral literature of tribal enclaves was as significant as the written literatures produced by academics. Singing with Asa on the tapes were Joe Abdo Sr., Quentin Bruguier, Lorenzo Dion, Duane Shields, Joseph Shields Sr., and Philomene Dion.

Asa was a marvelous teacher and told me he believed that

Yankton Peyote music comes from the sounds made by a special grass found growing on the prairie. The grass grows close to the bluffs and in the middle of August, particularly, when the hulls have turned dry and hot the grass makes a particular sound as you walk through it. When the Dakotas walk from one place to another, they take some of this medicine before they leave home and they concentrate on the meaning of power in the universe. There is a seed which had dried and a bird chirping and they stop and then it will come through the grass into your voice.

In composing the songs, he said, "we remember we are Dakotas and our days are good: *anpao wichakpe wiya u yak papka*, the Morning Star tells of that and how the stars connect everything including us to the earth." As he talked about composing, he also said that the language and the mythological knowledge of places of origin were crucial components of all oral literatures. When we walked out into the hills of Ihanktowan country along the roiling river so close to his house, we could often hear the slapping of water against the shore; he showed me how the songs came to him as he composed his own lyrics.

At this time he had other troubles. He was appealing his conviction for selling eagle feathers to an undercover agent of the U.S. government, but those problems were not part of his song. We talked at great length about the effort on the part of U.S. legal systems to "wipe us out." I donated some money for his legal defense.

As we walked, the air was a perfect, cool touch on my face, and he started to sing: *An pe-tu wo-wi-yu skin en.* We both knew this simple song because we had both been raised in the Yankton-Santee tradition of the Christian church, so I joined him, timidly: *Wa kan tan ka ma yu ha ye.* We walked toward a vacant, falling-down house where he said he had lived as a child. "It's gone now," he said. "But the songs are still here." I had a notion to take hold of his arm but knew it would be intrusive and impolite. He walked a few steps ahead of me and fell silent. I didn't want to attract the scavengers near the foothills of the river, and I didn't want to break the absolute breathlessness of the moment, so I just trailed along.

When I wrote this profile for the journal, telling of the sacred places and traditions and the efforts to maintain them, I thought this might be a permanent feature of the magazine. But like a lot of good ideas, it fell away simply because I had no time to continue traveling to write and interview. Besides, Asa accepted a consultant job with an eastern church school and became more and more evangelical.

In spite of some unfortunate omissions concerning the oral literatures that are so much a part of the creative process for tribal writers and artists, I was proud of the journal's beautiful layout and the covers donated by Native artists of my acquaintance, proud of the editors who contributed material and their scholarly credentials for our first issue and for the next ten years that we continued to publish at EWU. The journal has flourished and is still edited and published by the Arizona State University Indian Studies Department and the University of Minnesota Press under the editorship of Dr. James Riding In, Pawnee.

The major contributing editors in the beginning, now called the founding editors, were Dr. Beatrice Medicine, Dr. William Willard, and Professor Roger Buffalohead. Buffalohead was rather more of a silent partner, but Willard and Medicine were very active editors throughout the years until the journal went to the University of Minnesota Press and editorial offices in ASU, Tempe. It continues to thrive under the editorship of James Riding In, a scholar who has become a lifelong friend of mine; one of the reasons being that he, unlike many other historians, does not blame the powerful Sioux Nation for what is now called Pawnee historical grief land theft and other grievances. "It's the U.S. Cav.," he says with a knowing smile, "the military, the department of interior, federal policy . . . et al." His writings prove his point.

When the journal began and developed, it was a thrilling moment for all of us who wanted to write. It is a fact that editors become editors because they want to have control over the academic publishing matters they consider important. After years of trying to say in my writing and teaching that the course of American racism and imperialism was the cause for massive land thefts and endemic poverty, social chaos, and death to indigenous peoples, I finally had a magazine at my disposal, and I looked forward to each issue.

This was a scholarly journal that would eventually reach all of the important Native repositories in the United States, as diverse as the New York Public Library and Sinte Gleska University Library, as well as repositories in fourteen foreign countries. In my view, this journal has had a significant influence on the direction of the discipline of Indian studies.

It was Vine Deloria Jr., though, who had academic instincts more profound than most of us. His take on what a journal of this kind could and should do was thought-provoking. He was unhappy that we just took whatever came across the desk, culling the articles that were pertinent to the discipline and sending the irrelevant stuff to file no. 9.

"What you need to do," he advised, "is 1) choose research topics, 2) assign Native scholars to do the research, 3) pay them, and 4) publish their work."

Oh, the power of cheese!, I thought to myself.

What I would have given for that possibility! That requires more academic support than we ever achieved and a substantial budget and younger editors willing to do the work.

However, wanting to direct the dialogue and be in charge was still the best trait I have displayed as an editor. This editorial trait to which I will readily confess may have come out of my childhood, where I was the youngest in the family, always the last in line with no clout at all, a girl-child with no obvious potential and many boy-cousins and an older brother who was called Chunskay. Older brothers aren't called that in Dakota Sioux families simply because they are older brothers. The name implies "first-born son," "know-it-all," and, yes, even sacred authority.

I use that as an excuse. The truth is I have deliberately and with malice-aforethought made enemies over the years with my writing and my claimed authority and my need to be in charge over the writing that I consider significant. I have written many poison-pen reviews of books I don't like, even though my considerate friend Dr. Mike Wilson has encouraged me to do as he does: "Liz, I write reviews only of books I like." I find that absurd, even though I recognize that he was pointing out the arrogance of my stance and attitude. Perhaps Mike is more of a poet than he acknowledges; most of the poets I know share his view.

This trait of mine of claiming authority was the cause for the breakup of one of the most important friendships of my long life and the intellectual collaboration between Dr. Beatrice Medicine and me. Bea and I were fast friends for many years. We traveled together, camped together at powwows, went to Sun Dances together in support of the people, dug ti(n)psina out on the prairie, cooked corn soup, drank many a glass of scotch and water, and danced the latest "white-man" dances in convention hotels everywhere, even the funky chicken. We would sit in our living rooms and talk endlessly into the night. We called each other younger sister and older sister in the traditional way. She was a well-known Native anthropologist, a role model for my daughters, and someone who often gave me good advice and assurance.

That is, she was until I published my critical views on the book written by Dr. Michael Dorris, her adoptive son, who claimed to be of Modoc heritage and taught at Dartmouth College. His book was called *The Broken Cord* (Reed, 1975), and it took up the matter of maternal alcoholism, Native women, and the consequences of the consumption of alcohol to fetuses, a syndrome called fetal alcohol syndrome. I told Bea I was going to review the book critically because I saw it as a serious attack on Indian women, and she said, "Do what you have to do." We both thought we could survive it, but we could not.

Dorris had adopted three Indian children from the Crow Creek Indian Reservation, where I was born and where I am still a landowner and the keeper of my parents' wretched house where I was raised. Dorris, whom I met only once, claimed to be unaware at the time of the adoption that these children had suffered from alcohol exposure in the womb; those of us who knew the family, though, knew of the trouble. Dorris said it was only later that he had investigated, to his horror, the abusive conditions of their lives on the reservation and the abuse of and by their mother, who died of alcoholism.

There were many reasons for my acid-pen review of *The Broken Cord*, among them my feeling that this was a misogynistic book that blamed Native women and would bring them harm on the home-lands. I was right about that; a young woman I knew from Fort Thompson Agency was arrested in her home by the tribal police, indicted for criminal behavior, and given four years in the federal pen for "endangering her baby by breast-feeding while under the influence." She lost custody of the baby, and her two older children were taken away from her by law. She did her hard time, has not seen her children since, and now lives by herself in isolation on the reservation, somewhat shunned by her relatives. No one knows where her children are.

My essay on *The Broken Cord* appeared in my 1996 collection of essays *Why I Can't Read Wallace Stegner*, ten years after Dorris had won the National Book Critics Circle Award for his "study" or "memoir." Reviewers across the country from the *Boston Globe* to the *New York Times Review of Books* said his book was like "a prayer from the heart." It was a long time before a *Nation* editor named Katha Pollitt wrote that the book illustrated a dangerous attack on Native women. I feared, as Pollitt pointed out, that the book would be used to incarcerate and intimidate Native women. And it was for several years until the legal mandate for endangered women was reshaped in tribal enclaves.

Beyond this danger, though, was my notion that such children as those Dorris adopted were "vulnerable subjects," to an adoptive father who was trying to make a name for himself in academia. Much later, *Vulnerable Subjects* was the title of a study on "ethics and life writing" published by Cornell in 2004 by G. Thomas Couser, a professor of English at Hofstra University. Couser calls this Dorris work a memoir, though many people thought it a study by a Native anthropologist. It was eventually revealed that Dorris's claim to be an Indian was insupportable, a dilemma during those days that contributed to the questions of who should write about Indians, who should write about the black experience, who should write feminist works. Essentialism became the prime focus.

Whatever the case, Cynthia Ozick, who wrote "Who Owns Anne Frank?," a critical analysis of the all-male response to women's issues that seemed pervasive at the time, said, "Fatherhood does not confer surrogacy." Women writers as well as others have suggested that the manipulation of subjects by powerful writers needs to be critically examined.

For me, this work was not a family memoir, and I wrote about it in a critical way. It is an ethnography, reminiscent of colonial ethnography by an anthropologist who calls for political action, predicting a communal catastrophe, another "death to the tribes" kind of sad horror. It expressed the Native American predicament of alcohol consumption by childbearing women in much the same way that *Black Elk Speaks* (University of Nebraska Press, 1932), a book by John Neihardt, discusses the loss of religion and culture (the "broken hoop" dilemma) as an end-of-the-line vision of absolute precariousness to the survival of Indians. The *Black Elk* work, by a scholar at the University of Nebraska, may be read as the ultimate prediction of disaster and death of an entire people. Dorris's book called for incarceration of Indian women for a nine-month period as a last-ditch effort to save the people from themselves. Neither book, especially not the Neihardt book, gives solace if the objective is survival of a people. These writers do not point to the colonial governing systems of the indigenes (called genocidal systems by some) as the reasons for such dilemmas resulting in death to an entire people. There is little critical examination of the real culprits to Indian life on reserved homelands, such as the oppressive cultural, economic, educational, and political systems.

Couser's concern, and mine, was with the "ethics" of representing "vulnerable subjects" whom he describes as "persons who are liable to exposure by someone with whom they are involved in an intimate or trust-based relationship but are unable to represent themselves in writing or to offer meaningful consent to their representation by someone else" (*Vulnerable Subjects*, 4).

In today's literary milieu, such writings abound, often called exposés, and they often make the bestseller list of the *New York Times*. This reality is hardly the appropriate source of professional ethics for a memoir written by someone who claims to be a scholar.

I am just a writer whose credentials as a scholar are skimpy indeed. Having said that, I must admit that writers often go beyond ethics, just as scholars do. Thus, none of us is blameless. I had known for years that my friend Bea had "in the Indian way" adopted Michael Dorris, whom she had gotten to know when she taught in the Indian studies program at Dartmouth, where Dorris was the chairperson. At this time, we are told, Dorris and his first adopted son "bonded as Indians," and they received their Indian names from the Medicine family who reside at Wakpala, South Dakota. Because of this, Bea told me not to ever expect that she would renounce that, and, surely, I did not.

I am a Dakota wiyan, too, born and raised by precise and mature people on the homelands, so no one had to tell me of the binding nature of these ceremonials and the possibility of my own breach of tribal ethics of the Dakota/Lakota/Nakota Nation when I wrote what I was compelled to write about the matter. These ceremonials, after all, are sacred.

After Beatrice read my book, she never spoke to me again and wrote me a letter saying she wouldn't. Our days as sisters had ended. She died unexpectedly some years later even while I thought we still had time on this earth to make amends. Her silence has been an open rebuke, a burden, an omnipresence.

How to behave as a Native scholar and at the same time as a Native person with obligations to a legacy as old as the earth is not something to be taken lightly. Both Bea and I had discussed this dilemma when we utilized the text called *The Tewa World* (University of Chicago Press, 1969) written by our colleague Dr. Alfonso Ortiz, a Native trained in anthropology. We had come to a personal agreement that such writing was fraught with ethical issues. Ortiz, a Native-language speaker, had written of religious matters concerning his Pueblo people, exposing what was thought to be tribal knowledge made available only to and for ancestrally designated holders and keepers of such knowledge. Once when I had the gall to try to use this text in a course I taught at Arizona State University, my Pueblo students got up and walked out on me.

Very simply, ethical behavior in indigenous thought is based in collaborative relationships with humans and the earth and the earth's creatures, that is, culture and environment. Native ceremonial life is the method by which these legacies are told and honored and made useful.

Life writing, on the other hand, is the generic category to which autobiography and memoir belong and is of particular concern these days since it is a fact that underrepresentation of the marginalized lives of those such as former slaves, Native Americans, "nobodies," victims, and those with disabilities has been taken up in the American scholarship of many disciplines, including anthropology. In the latter part of the twentieth century, there has been a memoir boom, and such writing has become accessible as never before.

The last year before my final retirement (I've retired more times than Cher!), I taught an ethics class at Arizona State University in Tempe with twelve young Native undergraduates, all of them born and raised on the Indian reservations of the Southwest, many of them speaking their own tribal languages.

In this course we took up the responsibilities of those people trained in American scholarship, and particularly Indian people trained in the disciplines. The class was an experiment, and as such it may have been the only class in ethics taught in Indian studies anywhere, to undergraduates, and I think it has not been taught at ASU since. We had a strange and wonderful time reading and thinking about the ethics of the many who have written about Indians. I gave everyone an A in the course based on a final paper; this may have been another breach of ethics of a different kind but that class jerked me out of the absurd disillusionment that the pompous moral relativist has any answers.

My students' comments, their writings, and the books they brought me to read probably have given substance to the idea that I should not write a memoir, since I have for years condemned the memoir as a notoriously dishonest genre, irrelevant, boring, unethical, and wrong!

It is remarkable that I am now writing a memoir. The ethics of how to do this came out of the discussions I had with my students in that class, when they seemed to agree that people should probably not indulge themselves by writing memoirs. They considered such works in contemporary Native literatures, at least, to be self-centered and irrelevant and exploitive, and I agreed. The writing of memoirs may be very simply, an indulgence. More, it is probably a misunderstood undertaking.

Dorris's work was not, I suppose, meant to be a classical memoir, though most of us agree that memoirs can be what they want to be. Much of his work on the subject of his children seemed to mix rather unsatisfactorily two very different genres: that of a science scholar (anthropology, psychiatry, and counseling) and the sad remembrances of a troubled parent. What broke my heart about the Dorris story, though, was when he said, "By all evidence, he [Adam, the son] had been deprived of the miracle of *transcendent imagination, a complex grace that was the quintessence of being human*" (*Broken Cord*, 167). What? What? Because he has deficiencies, he is not human? This kind of arrogance toward someone you love and who loves you is unbearable.

8

WRITERS ARE WRITERS, THOUGH, and often we do engage in works that are all those things my students said they were. Sometime after I reviewed the Dorris work, in 2002, I got an award from the Mountain Plains Library Association for my "literary contribution" to the history of the Mountain Plains region. To this day, I don't know what initiated this award, since I'm not a historian, have done very little teaching in the Northern Plains, and, more significantly, there has not been much institutional recognition of my work.

In retrospect, I guess I can thank Dr. W. Marquardt and Dr. C. Woodard of my alma mater, South Dakota State University in Brookings, for my nomination, as both were at that time involved in the South Dakota humanities groups as well as the university library acquisitions, corresponding with me concerning many topics, including donating my papers to the university library there.

When I drove to Fargo, North Dakota, to accept the award, I found when I got there a room filled with dozens of people who were also recipients, and we were encouraged to give very brief responses to this distinct honor or no response at all. Thus, I said very little in thanks for the recognition.

"Two minutes," they told us was the limit. The title of the award banquet and conference was Exploring New Pathways to Information, so finding a Plains Indian writer born and raised on the reserved lands of the Sioux was, probably, an incentive for the libraries to take note of my work. I knew no one at the conference and spoke to no one about how I had become a recipient. In 1997, though, when my first collection of essays, *Why I Can't Read Wallace Stegner*, came out, the book had gotten notice for the Gustavus Myers Award for the Study of Human Rights, so that little-known award, too, may have influenced my inclusion in the library award.

At any rate, this library notice gave me occasion to think about my writing and publishing, which had started rather late in my life. I published nothing until I was forty and thought of myself as a very obscure writer of quite limited associations. At other times, when I appeared on panels and was asked who I thought my audience was, I always answered that I didn't have a clue and that, in fact, I was often astonished to know that I had an audience of any kind. I'd never had an agent and was damn lucky to find some editors who were interested in what I had to say!

About that time, I happened upon the work of a writer who was born and raised in Fargo, North Dakota, by the name of William H. Gass, a philosopher and teacher whose collection gave me some place to go with these thoughts. In Gass's *Finding A Form*, he says, "There are few vocations (like writing and the practice of poetry, for example), that are so uncalled for by the world . . . so unremunerative by any ordinary standards." He is right, of course, which means that I, like many others, have been grateful for whatever notice our work has received.

All of us who are writing and practicing poetry and trying to make sense of the world through our scholarship know Dr. Gass is right. The world pays us little mind unless we are going to write a melancholy and ahistorical *Dances with Wolves* about freeze-dried Indians and put it on film. If the work done by library associations and historical and literary societies pays attention to our obscure stuff, it means somebody is paying attention and we don't have to slash our wrists if what we desire is some meager notice.

For the most part, Dr. Gass's remarks cannot be denied. There is nothing so unrewarding as a writing career unless what you like most in the world to do is write. The other day someone asked me, "What does your family say about your writing, you know, your children, parents, loved ones?" Very little, actually.

What I've found is that a writer who wants to talk about his or her writing—the writing itself, I mean—is viewed sort of in the same way one would view a discussion of a rather persistent case of herpes. This is not a personal observation on my part; indeed, Dr. Gass may have given it to me as a genuine metaphor. But your need to write is here and then it is there and then it is gone and forgotten and then it is back, bothersome and even painful.

As a writer, one is dying to talk to someone about the work one does, the work that, as it is often said, makes one's soul an articulate thing. We imagine the world knows us and it cares, but in the end we are alone. We are alone. Writing is one of the few vocations that requires you to spend countless hours and days and weeks mucking about in your own silence, in tilting your own windmills, without help, without group consensus, unaccompanied, undisturbed, and, finally, facing your own firing squad.

Well, this sounds rather dismal, doesn't it? But on the other hand, let me say this, *I love writing.* I've never believed nor said with any confidence, "I want *to be* a writer." What I've said is, "I want to write." There is a huge difference.

I don't kid myself that I am a great writer, not even a good one sometimes. What I do know is that carefully using the power of words makes me, and all of us who try, into better human beings, and if we get efficient enough at composing language as something more than mere marks on a page, the words themselves have their own precious lives not to be thrown down as waste matter, and we can, perhaps, say what we mean. I know of few other human activities that can do that.

Being a Dakota Sioux Indian writer, though, from a community in which all conflicts are regulated by consensus, is something I've had to struggle with. Stifling myself is not easy. Aggressive and conversational politics, not consensus, is my pleasure, and it is ironic that I have never accepted the repressive language that was introduced to me in my youth and that I oddly hold dear. Now a bit long in the tooth, I recognize that patterns of the male-oriented dialogues of a family of men who thought of themselves as political people concerned about how they and their people were governed. I did not grow up smart, but I grew up reading everything that came my way, and after a while I realized that writers can give you good advice, such as when Gass says, "*irony* is often the only possibility of rebellion for the intelligentsia."

Words are to be cherished, even written ones. I remember when one of my grandmothers would hear us, her bilingual English-speaking grandchildren, use words carelessly or unintentionally insulting to each other, she would say: "Iya pi he sni. Dak ota iapi tewa h(i)nda." (Do not talk like that. We love to talk Dakota.) I didn't know it at the time, but what she was doing was helping us to understand the sacredness of our use of language. She spoke carefully, always, and used words as though they were illustrations of how the human mind works. From her I learned that using words is not just a grubby, tiresome, obsessive, awful, and obscene way to save our grand and arrogant selves. It's not like the banality of the supermarket tabloids that tell lies for profit; it's not like listening to the insanity of HBO where anything goes. It's not just telling our stories, or fulfilling our teacher's assignment, "what I did during my summer vacation." It is much more relevant to the human condition than that! Indeed, using words well helps us to put a face on the literary responsibility we have to each other. To care about words is not just to pass along the message. It is to develop out of culture and politics a critical conscience that helps us to know how to walk many paths, yet choose the right one.

Some time back I wrote a little essay about writing and reading and learning. I called it "How Scholarship Comes to Be Relevant." It was about growing up on the Crow Creek in the late thirties and forties in a place and time where there were no books to read, no libraries. No libraries! It was a time when I knew very few who wanted to talk English and certainly not read in English, let alone write it. On the reserved lands of the people, 350,000 acres, there were no libraries! No one there attended Harvard or read at the London Museum. We had only our own intellectual curiosity to catch up and find out about the other worlds, the literate worlds, and we did that by listening to the radio, going to the churches for reading materials, and telling one another the stories.

We subscribed to almost nothing in terms of journals and magazines, but I personally read everything I could get my hands on from school. There was a collection of books at a library in a neighboring off-reservation town called Chamberlain, and we sometimes went there. Newsstands like those you see in university towns were not available to rural populations like ours in those days and, sadly, still aren't.

Library and book deprivation was a real thing, and it still goes on in the places that are important to me, except now there is the ubiquitous television and Facebook. I've become more depressed than ever when I recognize that democratic regimes are only interested in the money. That means if we have been conned into believing that Borders Books is really a bookstore we are naïve believers in fantasy and facile entertainment and we deserve a restless and ignorant generation.

To be fascinated about the many processes by which humans find answers about the universe is to know that it starts in language. It starts with words. Now I know that some people today say it starts with pictures and sound. The truth is it still starts with writing, which is, as my friend Ray Young Bear defines it simply, " the experiment with words." He is a Mesquakie tribal language speaker who writes deeply artistic English prose and is one of the most fascinating, careful, sensitive writers on the contemporary tribal scene.

I stopped sending out my poems for publication years ago. It was sometime after I published a book of poetry called *I Remember the Fallen Trees*, and people really thought it was a collection about trees. And nature. Poetry is the genre to which I am most sensitive, and unlike my response to the rejection of my nonfiction, which I take rather off-handedly, I can't stand the rejection of my poems. Such comments as "we do not think that it fits with our list," or "unfortunately, due to the volume of submissions . . . ," or "we are not taking on new clients" are too numerous to mention.

One editor wrote, "I am sympathetic, but not convinced," as though I were a welfare recipient or slightly needy. I'm telling you now, such awful, pitiful responses are unworthy of my amazing and agonizing and ponderous efforts. I've kept writing poems; I just don't send them out to anyone, anywhere . . . except to a few special friends. One exception was when I sent a couple of poems to the Nimrod International Journal's Pablo Neruda Prize for Poetry thinking I might have something in common with those poets. I am no longer waiting for a response. Neruda, like so many of the South American poets, was a bureaucrat, a philosopher who had a critical mind, and, like Miguel de Unamuno, knew that prison (and blindness) both were good places for writers. Culture and politics are linked in South American literatures so that stereotypes can be examined.

I have never taken nor taught creative writing courses, which means, one supposes, that I don't know what poetry is and what so-called imaginative writings really are. I am reminded, therefore, that many others don't either. James McAuley, an Irishman who ran the creative writing program at Eastern Washington University for twenty years and author of several collections of poetry, liked to share this story:

"A young coed came to my office this morning and timidly said to me, 'Mr. McAuley, I want to register for your *imaginary* writing class.'"

"'No! No, missy,' I said, 'imagin-a-*tive*, imagin-a-*tive*!' She just stood and looked at me." The professor went back to Ireland shortly after that, and few of us have heard from him since.

Most of us who talk about writing and actually do writing (poetry and fiction in particular) get a big blast out of this kind of episode, not only because we live boring lives molding away in our offices grading papers, when every now and then someone like this delightful student will show up to enliven our grim chores, but because we recognize the contrived nature of what we do.

Yet to suggest, as this student does, that our work and our words and the classes we teach are *imaginary*, existing only in our own imaginations, is the final blow! The idea that our work means nothing, is even *imaginary*, leaves us vulnerable but with a hardness of heart that is difficult to bear. If you didn't laugh, you'd cry! Enough said about poetry.

At my age, thinking that I must do serious stuff, I am astonished to find myself in the throes of memoir-abilia. The issues of why we write and what writers (who are not imaginary) can do about whatever faces thoughtful people has become more important to me, so I have tried to get good at it. It has taken me forever to use English well. As I've said, I didn't publish anything until I was forty. And now, more than forty years later, I am reduced to writing memorabilia, that which might be "worthy of remembrance," as they say. Who am I kidding?

That American writers are influenced by whatever is in the news, drifting from one media flower to the next, sucking the honey of the moment for a hive of work that might sweeten the public's interest, was brought home to me once when I went to a reading by a poet from Dublin who was asked by an American student, "What have you found in Washington State that you might write about?" His answer: "nothing."

The question signified that the student thought the present surroundings, the flight in on United Airlines, the modern campus filled with statues and architecture, the latest fads in dress or hairstyle might be subject matter for poetry. His answer told her that for some writers fleeting surroundings are not enough. For some writers, politics and place and roots are more rewarding.

Many writers throughout the ages have gone to foreign lands to find subject matter. That's what Alexis de Tocqueville was doing when he arrived from France in America to tell the world of our shortcomings.

Presently (and for the last fifty years), the Middle East is on the agenda for American writers interested in the contemporary political scene. This trend suggests that politics in the contemporary world may not be unworthy of the attention of our most important writers. The forming of Israel in the Middle East was an act of courage and salvation, some have said. Others, including myself, suggest that it was an act of aggressive colonization. It has become the subject matter for countless writers, poets, and scholars alike who want to argue the point. Because it was an act of colonization, it has engendered acts of resistance that have been long and devastating and that, some say, should have been anticipated. Much of my own writing, both my poetry as well as my scholarship, has been to try to understand not only colonization but the resistance to it.

Any American who has witnessed the Sioux Nation's resistance to the theft and occupation of its lands in the Northern Plains of America by the federal government, BIA officials, constitutional lawyers, Christians, and greedy white farming and ranching immigrants (and now American writers like the *New Yorker*'s Ian Frazier looking for subject matter) knows that such resistances are trying to fight off the prison, the torture, and the poverty that the indigene suffers when colonization is institutionalized on a grand scale.

It seems astonishing that these political subject matters have become so important to writers, since many of us had been taught that the era of colonization was either a benign thing characteristic of the pilgrims or that it was over, done. We in America study colonization as occurring from the 1700s and fading into the Industrial Age and the world wars. Only the victims have grown up without forgetting anything and have thus decided that politics is not beneath any of us in any genre of writing. Nor is it beneath the resistances that occur.

Unfortunately, much of what has been heard in this country about any colonial act, whether toward Indians or Arabs, is that the resistance to it by the Arab population being displaced and murdered is an unexpected and unaccountable evil that will, surely, come to its righteous end; that what is going on is not colonization per se but progress. It is often described in defensive terms for democracy. The first decade of the twenty-first century has been a period of outrageous propagandizing about all that. The resistance to American Indian colonization has been swept under the rug of national discourse and is portrayed as the work of misled, unworthy, anti-American militants identified in such distractions as the American Indian Movement leadership. This has resulted in many more colonizing adventures.

This may be because writers have until recently failed to protest the collaborative stories between the major colonizer nations and their claimed powers. The rationalization of this has always been to transform a people under the impact of the West using the code name of *democratization* toward a morality that clearly, if we examine the history of the past one hundred years, cannot be sustained. In spite of the detractors, the so-called third world made up of protesters has come into its own, and the writings of many scholars are being read in all venues.

When the American-raised prime minister of Israel, Golda Meir, talked of the forming of Israel in the beginning, she certainly did not talk of it as a colonizing act, though many knew that was what it was. That little piece of landscape has become a satellite to the West in the midst of unwilling and protesting Arab histories and non-Christian and non-Jewish civilizations.

Meier thought only of the Jews, and she clearly believed that Palestinians did not exist and that Arabs, in general, were untouchables. Her attitude was that there is no such thing as a Palestinian, a political and economic view that prevails today in much of the West. It's a little like the textual emergence of the stories about Indians on the north prairies of America that capitalists and democratizers chose to occupy, saying, "This is empty country. There were no people here." Terra nullius, it is called. If there are no people, what you have is a wilderness, and it is up for grabs.

I once visited a house dedicated to Golda Meir on the campus of Metropolitan University in Denver, Colorado, where she had been a youthful student and where she today is honored as a most treasured global statesperson. There is not a word there about the occupation and colonization she led, which still goes forward in the twenty-first century. Where the Palestinians on the West Bank and the Gaza Strip are almost invisible, one thinks of the Oklahoma Land Run of 1893, when immigrant settlers were let in to grab what they could of the Indian estates. History does repeat itself.

There is little reliable news. We are often told that the Israelis these days close their places to investigative journalists for their own protection. It is a way, of course, to silence anyone who disagrees with the story. Certainly, a monument to Golda Meier in America is a credible example of U.S. complicity.

Even though Gideon Levy, an investigating writer and Jewish man in the twenty-first century, has not been able to enter many of the forbidden places along the shores of Israel, he has now written a book called *The Punishment of Gaza* (Verso, 2010) and has decided, after throwing off the indoctrination of his Jewish past, that the Palestinian homeland is "the largest prison on earth." He has almost lost hope in the idea that colonization and occupation can be called a humanitarian undertaking for any of the participants.

In reading Levy's work, I want to cry out: there are prisons elsewhere too. And they are large. Indeed, there are nine Indian reservations in South Dakota, making up hundreds and thousands of acres of treaty-protected lands that are locked in the economic and cultural grip of colonization as dramatic as any place on earth. Such colonizations that Levy and I and many others speak of these days are the central dramas of much of the world and America in particular, where no one really takes responsibility for the historical crimes committed in their names, yet many bemoan the tragic poverty, the lack of housing, the loss of land that is the center for cultural life and the sorrowful future faced by the children. They step up to adopt the children they believe to be orphans and bring used clothing for them to the Christian churches that are, ironically, the initiators of such colonization everywhere in today's world. Little is said about the possibility of the return of stolen land so that tribal people might develop an economic system to support themselves, and there is even the malevolent suggestion that Indians should be grateful that Christianity and *civilization* was brought to them.

The price they paid for that and are still paying is enormous. In a twist of logic, Indians themselves have become the foreign presence in the land of their ancestors, while the invader thrives and pushes toward anything that is not tainted with the reality of what has been done to the unhappy indigenes in terms of imprisonment. Most American lawyers offer little solace because it is their charge to defend the U.S. Constitution, which as we know, was written solely for white male property owners. The delusions that these lawyers have suffered from since the 1885 Crow Dog case and the 1903 Lone Wolf case are that the forced invisibility of Indians and the confidence of the righteousness of the Constitution brings joy to all who live in the "land of the free and the home of the brave."

It is not only delusion; it is self-induced hypocrisy, fraud, and crime. What seems to be interpreted from these cases is that the U.S. Constitution did not vest in Indians anything more than the right to breathe and the right to occupy lands they had owned for centuries and, further, that Congress has made provisions to assume control by breaking treaties and, in a touch of sweet irony, assuming a "trust" relationship. That is not very different from what the Jewish writer says about the history of the Jews, who hear the invaders claim, "we 'liberated' the territories, 'preempted' the terrorists, and 'preserved order.'" They might just as well have been talking about the massacres and the killing on the Northern Plains in 1880 of millions of

Indians, who were not called terrorists then, rather "savages." The difference may be in long-held treaty relationships.

Gideon Levy, this writer, astute in many ways, deludes himself not because he says that Israelis will never get it (about which he may be right) but because he says the solution is that the region must turn to international pressure from the United States. Turn to pressure from the United States? What? What? Has he read any American Indian history? Political science based in the treaties with the First Nations? Federal Indian policy materials? Apparently not.

The truth is many in the United States who look at the colonization of American Indians fear that Americans will never get it either, and they are certain that the United States cannot and will not be the arbiter in any such colonial milieu. Levy's optimism resides abroad with international pressure as a ticket to justice and the return of lands to victims of colonization. This leads only to more failure. He believes that only under the pressure of a wide boycott, particularly from the United States, will Israel save itself. Is he kidding?

Public pressure and education and goodwill have not brought the land back to American Indians, even while it is known that the Supreme Court in 1980 said the U.S Congress stole much of it (the theft of the Black Hills, for example), and even when it is known that without the land Indian life cannot be sustained. Some believe American Indians, like the Palestinians, will forever be imprisoned in a colonial system by others who want their wealth and resources. Why would Levy put his faith in one of the most powerful colonizer of them all, the United States?

This is not a rhetorical question. Rather, it demands an analysis by the Jews and the Palestinians themselves, and an answer for Indians too. Since the question of how the U.S. Constitution applies to tribal nations is rarely understood or interpreted by lawyers and judges fairly, how can we say that such democratic ideals that stem from that document will influence what happens to the Palestinians in the Middle East? Apparently, U.S. courts do not believe that tribal-nation powers originated with the tribal nation rather than with U.S. federal powers, even though there is language (yes, untaxed) in the Constitution that says so. Sioux Nation sovereignty was original, not created by the U.S. Constitution, yet laws are rarely written, interpreted, or adjudicated to subscribe to this reality, and the treaties that exist are ignored.

9

IT MAY SEEM REDUNDANT at this point to say that I live in a Northern Plains state (organized in a statehood structure since 1889) where nine Indian reservations have been in place since the early 1860s. These reserved places house thousands of Indians who, in spite of their long and ongoing tenancy in North America, seem to be thought of by many Americans who have been in America for only three hundred years as inconsequential, often called "minority" populations or "ethnics." I know of no traditional Native person who readily accepts that definition.

Many of these Native enclaves were, certainly in the beginning, set up as concentration camps or colonies governed by European overseers until the American Revolution. Some changes have occurred since then. The Crow Creek Reserve where I was born has existed as a treaty-invested enclave since 1863. Today, these enclaves are thought of as reserves or treaty lands or First Nations or other such titles. They have been invested through their connections to the U.S. government with sovereign treaty rights and have set up "self-governing" systems in the midst of a wholly new modern civilization that has claimed to own the land and its indigenous peoples in a "protectorate" paradigm. Mostly these governing systems were put in place so that the tribal people who lived there would have a way to communicate with their overseers.

My thinking and writing has been absorbed in the indigenous struggle against that kind of colonization, which means that my work remains the work of a "minority" writer. Colonial possessions governed by powerful nations have been the sources of political power and captive of the rich sources of raw materials throughout the globe for as long as anyone can remember. As I have written about this throughout my academic career, I have accepted the notion that I am not only a "minority" writer, I am also a "political" writer. That truth is probably one of the major reasons that I left my home state and my tribal homelands in the first place to seek a professional life, and it certainly is the major reason that after a more than twenty-year professorship elsewhere, which was a very satisfying and successful time, I returned to where my political heritage is alive.

In the past decade or so I have lived in Rapid City, where I am known to be active in the scholarship that is tribally oriented. I was invited to be a mentor for a tribal writer's group called the Oak Lake Writers' Society almost twenty years ago. The writers' group is associated with the tribal college movement as well as with South Dakota State University in Brookings, South Dakota, my alma mater. I have been a member of the American Indian Movement since its inception and have attended many of the so-called American Indian legal trials in this state and others. The State of South Dakota has had a long history of conflict with tribes since the 1960s. Ongoing tribal protests against its policy and the federal Indian policy that governs the colonial enclaves on tribal lands cannot be ignored if one is a writer.

While all of this may seem inappropriate to be included in a memoir, this kind of political activity has always been a major interest for me. These trials are the bare bones of an agonizing reality. The result of crimes said to have been committed by Indians during the 1970–1990 American Indian Movement era of protest have been the background for much of my journalistic work and several collections of essays. These supposed crimes, many of them unsubstantiated, are now more than forty years old. In any other venue, they may have been described as protests to colonization. In the Midwest they are described as criminal behaviors. The law enforcement community, as well as the American public at large, thinks of Indian reservations as "problem areas," just as they did when Indians became colonial subjects instead of treaty participants years ago.

These tribal nations governed themselves for centuries and believe that since the coming of the white man, treaties are the law of the land, and many of them have signed treaties with several foreign entities including the United States of America. They had previously signed accords with other tribal nations, and some of these most important alliances known to them are still part of their history.

Some historians believe that the Native peoples in America are unique in the world because they are among the few aboriginal peoples *in the world* who are still attempting to practice sovereign self-government in the midst of one of the most powerful imperial nations known to history.

In my lifetime, there has been little change in the perspective of Indian-nation citizens, who never gave up their right to tribal-nation citizenship simply because they were awarded U.S. citizenship. When the Indian citizenship law was passed in 1924, there was little notice on most reserved lands except for a communal gathering or two scheduled so that tribal leaders like my grandfather could announce in the Dakota language to the people, many of whom even then did not speak English.

Grandfather, who sometimes went by the name of Joseph Tatiopa, was a tribal councilman and had the obligation. I do not remember these occasions, but as he talked about it much later, he said that sometimes a state official showed up to wave some papers at the gatherings, but sometimes they did not. Tribal politicians may have made a speech or two, but otherwise, life went on as before, with Indians possessing dual citizenship since 1924.

Non-Indian immigrant populations that surrounded reserved lands, however, could probably have had a much different reaction. To make Indians citizens of the United States, whether they wanted to be or not the act was passed by an all-white Congress, as are all the laws affecting Indians), probably made white neighbors feel a bit safer, having lived through the pioneer days, Indian Wars, and cultural conflicts that come with the deliberate invasion of the lands of others.

To appreciate how unerring and how habitual it is that Americans think of Indian reservations as problem areas in this country, look no further than a recent 2010 Tribal Law and Order Act passed by the U.S. Congress and touted by white and Indian politicos as the best thing since sliced bread, to use a pervasive cliché. The headlines read: "Prosecuting Program Comes to Pine Ridge," and "Justice System Hopes New Approach Will Make Reservations Safer." A bureaucrat named Gregg Peterman, new to many on the reservation, had helped Russia develop a better criminal justice system, and it was announced that in that year he was going to Iraq and Afghanistan to help federal prosecutors develop "democracies." Now he was at Pine Ridge.

This plan was thought by some tribal leaders to be based in two fallacies: that Indian reservations are enclaves of criminal behavior and that continued colonial law and order, placed on treaty lands ever since 1890 when Sitting Bull was shot to death, would "improve the function of the tribal justice system." Such thinking goes into much of the legal wrangling that takes place between tribal and state governments.

Without any analysis of the consequences, it must be stated at the beginning that what is devised in this act is not a "tribal justice system." It is a federally run colonial law-and-order system placed on treaty lands. Its officers are hired by the feds, trained by the feds, paid by the feds, and given their authority by the feds. They are an accommodating arm of the FBI that has a presence on Indian lands as in no other place I can think of. There is little in the law-and-order system proposed here that recognizes and supports the long-standing values and customs of tribal nations, histories, or needs, not on any reservation in the United States and certainly not in South Dakota, where state law has tried to gain supremacy in the last thirty years, even, perhaps since the Major Crimes Act of the 1800s.

Second, and perhaps more important, Indian reservations and the people who live there are no more criminally inclined than any other population (in spite of what some statistics will tell you). Having said that, I want to assure my readers that I am in favor of decent law and order, not only on Indian reservations, but also in towns like Rapid City, where I live. In my work I have tried to put forth the argument that the Sioux, traditionally, have been a law-abiding people, paying attention to the laws of the tiospaye and their leaders, a strong, self-sufficient people who knew how to behave toward one another.

Lately, I've noticed that the Oyate have demonstrated what we may call a "learned helplessness" in our communities. I've noticed that if your husband beats you up, you call the tribal police rather than your tiospaye people of order. If your child runs away from home, call the police; if a relative comes over and makes himself obnoxious, call the police. These used to be called familial matters, not police matters, and they were often handled by parents, grandparents, men and women of the community who upheld the rules and regulations of the people.

It is important to ask the colonizing forces around us the serious question that this behavior demonstrates: who destroyed the ability of Sioux families and tribal communities to take care of their own?

Nowadays, if someone is selling dope in the community, there seems to be no alternative but to call the FBI, prosecute the offender, and send him to the federal pen for the rest of his life. If someone is drinking and driving, arrest him, give him three chances, and then send him to the pen for four years, put "felon" beside his name so he won't ever get a decent job and can't get money to go to school and get an education. In the fall of 2015, with "overwhelming support from the Oglala Sioux Tribal Council" (Pine Ridge Reservation), we were told a "pilot program" would be put on all reservations in South Dakota called the *community prosecution strategy*. It would put dozens of federal law enforcers on Indian lands. Big names in the Indian communities here, like Dani Daugherty, Tracey Fischer, Lisa Iyotte,

B. J. Jones, Sherman Marshall, Frank Pommersheim, Roger Campbell, and Tom Shortbull, were on board for this undertaking, and "liaisons" from the U.S. attorney's office in Pierre would be assigned to every tribal court. When I wrote about this furtherance of the clear and present colonial danger to Native nation sovereignty, no local newspaper chose to publish my article.

When I spoke to Dr. Ed Valandra (Sicangu), then head of the Indian Studies Department at the University of South Dakota, his cynical question born of Sicangu Sioux Indian experience on the reserved lands was, "Does that law overturn *Oliphant?*" The answer, we knew, was "no." We agreed that those unaware of this kind of legal history ought to consult the work of Vine Deloria and David Wilkins and change directives.

In our discussion we thought about the function of law and history and how there was so little change. "Who doesn't know," Valandra said, "that *Oliphant vs. Suquamish Indian Tribe* was the most anti-Indian judicial decision made in modern times?" That was decades ago, and it took away further law-and-order functions from the tribes. It held that tribal nations (without an express congressional delegation of power via treaty or congressional act) are precluded from trying non-Indians who commit crimes within reservations, even while some statistics tell us that most of the crime on Indian reservations is white on Indian rather than Indian on Indian, especially as it concerns the women's domestic violence and rape issues.

The *Oliphant* decision has had national impact even though it has since been amended. It emerged from a case brought by a teeny-weeny tribe in Washington State with forty-three enrolled tribal members and a land base about as big as my living room. The notion that a tribe with such a small land base should be the arbiter for those tribes in the West that possess hundreds of thousands of acres of land and have thousands of citizens is preposterous. This was a 1970s decision that clearly moved in the direction of termination for all tribes.

This legal stuff of 2010 is something I've written about over and over again, calling it a prosecutor's dream. Some scholars, like Wilkins, who teaches law and politics at the University of Minnesota, and even Valandra, along with so many other Native writers, make a big deal out of the moral principle of consent in the law, outlined in the Northwest Ordinance of 1787 as well as treaty law. I have taught that, too, as a moral principle. Yet I'm not sure that consent is the answer, since we seem to have tribal leaders and lawyers who sanction and legitimize opinions and ideas that reflect the ideas of the nontribal sector of our American population rather than the consent of the citizens of the tribal nation.

Often we, the tribal nation and the citizens of the tribal nation, are seen as a problem area, even by our own Native peoples who run the bureaucracies. Our values seem not to be shared by everyone because for us it is the family that makes up the nation. Family is the center of our strength. For the bureaucrats it is colonial law and order.

Of the questions I ask, three are significant: Does this new Law and Order Act strengthen the family or diminish it? What does it do for the issue of poverty on Indian lands, a major cause for conflict and chaos in any community? And what can we say about our future hopes for our children?

10

IN THOSE YEARS WHEN I found myself "professing" at Eastern Washington University, that time of great plans and dreams for those of us who had not had visibility in either the political or scholarly world for such a long time, national liberation movements were afoot across the land, and everyone was talking about peace and justice and equality and the end of poverty. What we did not want to notice underneath it all was a resentment that involved violence and minor disturbances and sometimes just pettiness. A Northwest Indian totem pole in the yard of our Indian studies office was deliberately cut down and defaced. Professors' tires were slashed. Little investigation occurred. Our student body was restless, but my work there was satisfying and life went on.

Just a few years before I retired, I noticed a huge change in the academic climate around the field of Indian studies. Once so filled with hope and enthusiasm, Indian studies was becoming the square peg, it seemed to me then. Such scholarship documenting the vicious colonization of American Indians and placed squarely in the classroom of an imperialistic nation that had been largely successful in hiding its own history of genocide, murder, and land theft was not well received in some areas.

What had once been a welcoming applause by a still-reluctant and admittedly hesitant academic world as a good idea, Indian studies and all of the scholarship surrounding what were called "minority" enclaves were falling into disrepute. It was not just a critical analysis of the flaws in emerging disciplines; it was a backlash against what people began calling the "multicultural left." The criticism was filled with resentment and was returning to the white supremacy in academia that many remembered.

What made Indian studies important at this moment in history was what it said about colonization. It asked what happens when colonial governments continue the oppression of Native people in a time of enlightenment. Law schools, in an effort to say that colonization of Indians in this country was and is a humane activity rather than a crime, were now trying to take over Indian studies departments, much as anthropology had risen to power in academia decades before. The plan was to give power to a disciplinary knowledge base in the law of reconciliation and assimilation. Non-Indian and Indian lawyers believe that an intellectual movement called postcoloniality can be achieved through forcing democracy upon these nations through the administering power of the United States, another process of colonial governance.

I had noticed this kind of resentment against Indian studies before, and it sometimes emerged even in my private life. Maybe it was just the culture of the city to be rude and inconsiderate and had nothing to do with my being an Indian. Yet I thought it was tied, in some vague way, to the unexpected responses to my Indian family when we moved into a college town called Cheney, inhabited mostly by white professional people, just on the outskirts of Spokane, Washington.

The resentment was a strange mixture of impatience at our very presence and resignation, highlighted in an exchange I had with my landlady when I complained that the screen door of my rental house was in need of repair. I had called several times, and when she finally showed up, she said, "Well, it's probably better than living on the reservation, isn't it?"

I usually ignored these kinds of insults, but they were and still are ubiquitous. Years later, when my grandson moved from Albuquerque to South Dakota and enrolled in one of the city schools, his counselor asked, "Why don't you enroll at a school on the reservation?"

"Because I don't live there," he said with his usual calm logic.

When he told me about it, I said sarcastically, "Welcome, son, to the lands of your ancestors."

In my early years at EWU, when I still seemed to be barely feeling my way around, not yet a member of the club, I found myself standing in the faculty coffee room one cold morning. It was in the spring of the year I was up for tenure in an English department where I taught classes and had a dual appointment in Indian studies.

Clutching my coffee cup and getting ready to go to my office to meet students, I was told by a smiling, convivial male colleague who was also up for tenure in the same department, "Hey, you won't have any trouble getting tenure. After all, you fit two categories. You're an Indian. And you're a woman."

This was a man who had migrated to the Northwest from England, became an American citizen some twenty years before, and now taught Shakespeare and Chaucer to receptive American students. He was a brilliant scholar, one whom I thought of as a friend, and one who had always been a member of the club if for no other reason than his beautiful British accent. I murmured something about a good morning and went down the hall feeling quite inadequate, even though I had even at that time a reasonably good publishing vita and excellent student reviews. Fitting two categories? I suppose it's better than fitting none. These matters seem petty when one considers that some countries around the world put to death their dissenters.

The massive and more obvious resentment that came later might have been one of the reasons for my early retirement. The drift of the national debate on these matters had gone beyond resentment and had entered a vicious stage. Even today that debate has not diminished; note the 2009 Arizona political rejection of government funding to state universities for minority, ethnic, or multicultural studies. Those departments are not just being diminished; they are in many cases being wiped from the face of academia. In the most recent political scene, associates are still complaining about discrimination against whites brought about by what is called affirmative action.

Even worse is the tendency to appoint in Native studies departments non-indigenous scholars who are credentialed in colonial studies or American studies, without caring how necessary it is to bring into the academy the Native people who need and want to study themselves as indigenous and isolated populations, not settlers nor colonizers nor immigrants. Nowadays, white scholars with little knowledge beyond the barriers of the mainstream are heading up the departments and programs called Indian studies, and they do it with straight faces.

Who is to say with authority, then, what is progress in academe? In 1988 the Ivies had decided to include what they called third-world authors in their required curriculum. *Required* is the key word here. Franz Fanon would be required now, just as Virgil, Kant, Freud, Hawthorne, and Shakespeare were required at Stanford University in Palo Alto, California. Edward Said's texts on colonization of indigenous peoples were assigned. It was a precedent-setting move by one of the elite universities of the land, and it did not go down well with the defenders at the gates of academe. The uproar was heard up and down university avenues, and many indigenous texts were disparaged by the faithful elite even while this integration occurred.

This is not to suggest that every text written by an indigenous or "third-world" author is worth the inclusion, nor is the massive cutting down of trees for the paper to print them in any way justified. There is a huge list of works written by so-called deconstructionists that does not deserve our attention. If one were to read some of the poetry of people who have gotten wide attention, one would have to admit that *doggerel* is still a useful term in literary criticism. It's not just a matter of taste, nor is it just a matter of "political correctness." It is a matter of the demands of scholarship.

I agree that much of the time, deconstruction amounts to simply making no distinction between the text itself and the biography of the writer. "Are you a real Indian?" was the first question I got on the telephone from a New York editor who published my first book of fiction, *The Power of Horses and Other Stories*. How does one answer that? What does that mean? What it means is that there are many imposters among us, and even New York editors are aware of it. That's a good thing, in spite of its ringing bias.

When Ian Frazier, a writer for the *New Yorker* magazine, met a Lakota man on the streets of Manhattan one weary day, he knew he had met a "real Indian," a Sioux Indian born and raised on the prairie homelands who talked the Lakota language and knew where he came from. This "real Indian" helped him write *On the Rez* (Farrar, Straus and Giroux, 2000). No matter that the man was daft and the book a travesty, the "Indian informant" was at least not an imposter.

The editor who asked me if I was a "real Indian" did not talk to me about the short story as genre nor about my little collection as an examination of what the American short story does so well—narrating of bits and pieces of ordinary life and, in the case of this collection, identifying forms of Indian resistance plausible in advanced capitalist and imperialist countries like the United States. What any worthwhile text divulges is the measure of its usefulness to the process of learning in a democratic society. The most egregious example of the backlash to indigenous scholarship happened as the memoir of a young Guatemalan Indian named Rigoberta Menchú Tum was being assigned with increasing frequency in university reading courses and not just in Indian studies or anthropology. It was becoming a major influence in English departments and politics and even law schools, as it told of the consequences of Guatemalan official response to a guerilla war being fought by peasants against the elites of a very undemocratic society. The consequence of the colonization of natural resources is poverty.

This was a memoir that documented the 1970s murderous purge by the Guatemalan military of hundreds of thousands of Indians with the explicit help of the U.S. political and military establishments. No one ever asked Menchú if she was a "real Indian," but they certainly questioned her right to narrate the history of her own country. I read the book and assigned it to students, but I must admit that I knew a lot more about the Northern Plains Indian experience with aggressive colonization than I did about South America until I read her story.

Later, truth commissions called the time written of by Menchú in her work a period of genocide caused by the effort to bring indigenous enclaves under state control so that the land and resources could be exploited and the people colonized. Isn't that always the function of imperial impulses in government? Even as we see the consequences of that thinking, we in America still teach our elementary students of the harmoniousness of the courageous pilgrims, the first colonizing settlers, who have been let off the hook through a colonial educational system. Our denial of colonization as genocide in this country is a profound mistake in light of today's global resistances taking place everywhere.

Menchú documented the killing of her parents and brother who were among the 80 percent of the population driven into starvation and homelessness as their villages were burned to the ground in a scorched-earth Guatemalan policy with U.S. financial support during the Ronald Reagan presidency.

Conservative, or some say right-wing, scholars took the stage during the period of Menchú's literary efforts. David Horowitz, a failed professor of politics whom my friend and colleague Dr. Oneida Meranto of the Metropolitan State College in Denver, Colorado, calls a "sinister individual," led the effort to degrade the scholarship of not only Menchú but much of the work being done during these years by indigenous or third-world scholars, including Meranto herself. Horowitz was then publishing an e-magazine and often appeared on conservative radio talk shows ranting about "liberal" professors who were brainwashing "our" students.

Though I don't usually read political science journals, I recently happened upon a piece by his nemesis, Meranto, called "The Third

Wave of McCarthyism: Co-opting the Language of Inclusivity," in *New Political Science* (vol. 27, no. 2 [June 2005]). Citing cases, she warns of the brainlessness of the attacks on university systems across the country from people like Horowitz, who has had much backing from right-wing supporters.

In understanding that this backlash is ongoing, Meranto tells of a much later appearance of Horowitz on Metropolitan's campus in Denver, and she does not mince words concerning the kind of propaganda spouted by a man she calls "a self-proclaimed red diaper baby." It was about this time that Meranto appeared on Horowitz's list of the "hundred most dangerous professors in America," which is, by the way, the charge toward Indian studies as a discipline often given by those who wish to dominate the dialogue as a propaganda instrument. This means that trying to tell the truthful stories of colonized peoples on this continent will surely bring on vituperation from conservative blabbermouths, but even more troubling, it will prevent the search for new meanings and solutions.

Horowitz called the book *I, Rigoberta Menchú* "a tissue of lies" and "one of the greatest hoaxes in the twentieth century," even as he was trying to get Meranto fired from her tenured position in Denver and as he slandered other moderate thinkers. He was not alone. As I remember the events of this time, an editor of my acquaintance forwarded to me a manuscript by Dr. David Stoll, an anthropology professor who had studied at Stanford and was now teaching at Middlebury College in Vermont, saying simply, "This might interest you." Stoll's manuscript appeared in my mail early on in the discussion of Menchú's work but ten years after she published her memoir and, surely, before I was fully aware of such an attack on Menchú as part of the culture wars to come.

This manuscript made the rounds of university press editorial offices in search of a publisher and was rejected by several of them who recognized Stoll's politically motivated agenda against indigenous voices. Stoll titled his manuscript *Rigoberta Menchú and the*

Story of All Poor Guatemalans and vigorously debunked the Menchú memoir as an exaggeration and distortion of the events. In doing so, he became the first mainstream academic to join the case of how memoirs can be used by unscrupulous right-leaning scholars with an agenda, giving biased arguments the veneer of academic respectability. I've always thought memoirs (perhaps even including this one) to be self-serving, but at the time I wondered why an indigenous memoir of real events was any more self-serving or biased or untruthful than any other.

I found the answer when I learned that Stoll had written for Christian-oriented outlets for many years before he became a part of the anthropology school of studying Indians, the discipline that had been engaged in a long and futile attempt to defend itself against Vine Deloria's barrage of charges in the 1970s about its practice of colonial handmaidenship.

No one knows what resentments Stoll may have stored up in his studies at Stanford, which was, like several other elite universities at that time, a hotbed of culture-war activity. Some sympathetic critics of his work on Menchú have suggested that he simply wanted to explain what he thought he knew of Guatemala's civil war and that he had every right to do so without being harassed by liberals or others. From his journalistic writings, he claimed close knowledge of peasant and Christian groups and believed them to be free of the anticolonial, anti-Christian, and anti-American ideology that he said was driving the war as well as informing Menchú's story. He believed that most Guatemalan Indians were *passive by their very nature*, not given to revolutionary methods. My experience tells me that the colonized are not passive, that they always recognize their condition of servitude, and often know how to hide what they know from "inquiring minds" like Stoll's. Nature usually tells us that passiveness in the face of colonization is not a natural condition. It may be a stereotype.

Stoll's perversity toward Menchú's work seems to claim elitist credentials, but his use of stereotypes concerning the Indians of

South America to explain one of the most important protests of the period is simply unacceptable. In addition to his bias, it is odd that as an anthropologist he seems to know very little about the function of memoir in historical or even literary terms. What he fails to acknowledge is that in the genre called memoir, the tactic of rearranging events and exaggerating traumatic events as Menchú may have done comes with the territory.

This trait does not mean that the suffering revealed in Menchú's story does not assist her readers in understanding the criminal nature of a fascist government toward its indigenes. What it means is that understanding the function of memoir should be taken seriously by cultural anthropologists, who are often visitors and tourists in indigenous enclaves, and should not be dismissed as wrong or too political or left-wing or any of the other descriptions that can be applied.

The Stoll fiasco reminds me of the bias often shown by white men and women who visit the Lakota/Dakota/Nakota reservations in the Northern Plains, sometimes for very long periods, even marrying into the tribe to become "experts" who then are called upon at every occasion to explain the Indian people they are observing. Their contradictory observations often become history even though they often go against the information given by those who have lived indigenous lives.

How else can we explain the fact that the Lewis and Clark diaries are often taken seriously as examples of American history to be revered and taught to our young even though they are the diaries of government agents who invaded western tribes with an aggressive colonial agenda in mind. Apparently, writing everything down in European languages makes experts. The real problem is that even Indians often recite these narratives as real, having lost their own sense of history through the constant barrage of information supported by white communities.

It has been observed by some critics that colonial-driven works often delve into a purist kind of American historiography that receives much agency in the scholarly world. Writers like the Pulitzer Prize-winning man of letters David McCullough, for example, whose book *1776* has received much academic acclaim, is an interesting cleansing of events. It is a good read even for someone like me, who has little interest in the specific subject matter. It's a page-turner, comparatively speaking, written in a delightful narrative style. Indians are, of course, absent, cleansing the inherent conflicts of history. No Indians? During the Revolutionary period? That is hardly explicable, unless you could get off a boat on the New England shores, wander inland and not see another living human being. This must have been the case, since only one complete page of the entire 380 pages is devoted to Native Americans.

Even though this book starts in England with the intention to explain America's protestations against His Majesty King George III, that is hardly a decent accounting or rationale for leaving out indigenousness as a concept of American history. Even in 1776, it seems to me, wars had to be fought and treaties with the indigenes had to be signed, which means there ought to be some mention of that reality by historians. The term *indigenous* rarely appears in histories of this kind.

McCullough tells us that George Washington did not want blacks in the army and certainly did not want Indians, who were fighting their own wars for survival in the colonies. He indicates that the war in 1776 was a "painful struggle" and that twenty-five thousand Americans were killed, but in this text at least, nothing is said about the forty years of Indian Wars, in which hundreds of thousands of Indians and many indigenous nations were wiped out.

The point is, America's historiography about its aggressive drive toward its own imperialistic power cannot be examined with any degree of authenticity as just the testimony of the brave and courageous epoch American writers and scholars are wont to claim. It can, perhaps, seem authentic when Indian Wars are not a major and essential part of the founding narrative because historians are anxious to get to the Civil War.

The issue of what is left out as the examination of the beginnings of America's rise to become a great nation is an essential matter in the development of Indian studies as an academic discipline, and that includes the critical analysis of historiography itself.

11

ONE OF THE MOST interesting of the theorists who wanted to make the Indian Wars an essential part of the narrative by delving into matters of history as well as indigenousness and politics and law was Vine Deloria, the Dakota Indian scholar born and raised in South Dakota. He was a brilliant man who ended up teaching at the University of Colorado in Boulder for many years and writing dozens of books for which he was *not* awarded the Pulitzer.

His books were among the first twentieth-century textual examinations of America's treatment of indigeneity as a concept that rose from the Northern Plains, the scene he believed was the locus of much of the crime. It is unfortunate that after his death, when he no longer has control of his own story, many white theorists and scholars have come out of the woodwork to proclaim him some kind of a spiritual guru, rather than the major Indian law historian who not only refuted America's falsified historiography but took on aggressive colonial anthropological studies enclaves as well. More significantly, he interpreted colonial law for what it was and is: the cause for wars and instability and death. He was among the first to deplore the use of the Bering Strait theory as an explanation of origins of indigenous peoples on this continent.

As proof of this new description of his work as spiritual rather than political, I give an example here, knowing it is only one of a dozen such efforts and knowing that I will again be called hateful, a scholar unworthy of university press publication, and, according to one critic of my acquaintance, "an unhappy woman." I'm none of those things. Yet in 2009 when I was invited to a symposium on this remarkable man's life and career, I began to wonder why I must be the constant critic.

The symposium, held at the Northwest Indian College in Bellingham, Washington, was entitled Philosophy, Spirituality, and Religion: A Tribute, and I immediately had a perverse reaction to the pietistic nature of the forthcoming discussion. Vine was not a public spiritual person so much as he was a public politician and law scholar. At the nearby Western Washington University in Bellingham, Deloria's private collection of books and some of his papers are reposited because he spent some of his early teaching years there. Many of us have gone there to peruse his stash. It's good reference stuff.

The day of the speech started for me at dinner with my often absent husband, who lived much of the time on his Spokane Indian Reservation near Wellpinit, Washington, a sort of pleasant rendezvous for us. CJ, my soul mate who never did think much of "togetherness," refused to live with me on an everyday basis, which meant that he lived in our log house on the Spokane Indian Reservation much of the time. We met for this rendezvous at the Northwest College campus, situated in the midst of the sumptuous lands of the Lummi Indians on the west coast of Washington, and as we were being served dinner, we began to discuss what I would say the next morning in my tribute at the fifth annual Vine Deloria Jr. Studies Symposium.

"Spirituality, huh?" CJ asked, chomping on his usual salad. He was a diabetic who learned a bit too late that *What you are is what you eat. And drink.* We usually ordered at restaurants with great care. "I thought he was a political writer," he ventured, while I, in a sadistic move, ordered a gin and tonic.

Knowing that we both had read everything Vine had ever written, I agreed, "Yeah, me too. I think it is because of a misreading of his first book, *God Is Red.* That book is *not* about religion, per se, though it is often thought to be. It is a political book that zeroed in on the politics of religion."

For the Bellingham symposium, the book entitled *C. G. Jung and the Sioux Traditions* (Spring Journal Books, 2009), was the centerpiece of the tribute to our distinguished honoree. Published posthumously under Vine's name, the book was edited by historian Dr. Philip J. Deloria, Vine's eldest son, and Jerome S. Bernstein, a Jungian analyst in private practice in Santa Fe, New Mexico, who says he never met Vine in person and the two of them had only a couple of telephone conversation before his death. Vine's wife, Barbara Deloria, holds the copyright to this book.

I knew I should tread this path carefully.

Yet as a writer myself, I consider any work published posthumously under the name of the deceased author a travesty, and this one in particular a repulsive violation of an important man's life and essential work, a transformation likely to have a ludicrous effect on his legacy. Bemoaning Western man's split from nature, as Jung did in his final years, is hardly enough for me to say that the editing of Deloria's point of view concerning "the primitive psyche" is anything but a sordid game played by those who want to benefit from his genius. It is not a tribute. It is an appalling psycho-trifling with the essential work of the most important political-legal Native voice of this century.

In spite of what some think of my aggressive reviews of books, I will refrain from further comment on the book itself. I have been taught to be polite, though I sometimes forget my mother's admonishments. It does tell me, even though I am not the major figure in scholarship that Vine was, that no matter how minor your voice may be, or how major it may be, it is expedient to burn your papers and notes and unfinished manuscripts while you can and refrain from thinking your last manuscript is likely to serve as the apostle of a true religion.

Politics, I've often said, is the discussion we have about how we are governed, and Vine's fame and protestations in that arena will never be matched in our lifetimes. Religion and philosophy, on the other hand, is what glitters and befuddles, and I think he knew that too. That is the case whether you are talking about Westchester County in the state of New York or about the Eagle Butte Agency in Sioux country or any of the hundreds of Native enclaves in America.

Politics is simply the conversation we have about how we are governed, and Vine's take on that was masterful! If you are talking about solutions to failed governance in the Indian world, you need to go to the colonial beginnings in law, as he did, not Native spirituality. The unfortunate reality of Indian history and law is that too often our discussions are examinations of our spiritual natures rather than the U.S. colonial law that has made us beggars in our own country. No one needs to know how we talk to God if what we want to do is to resist the theft of our estates.

Indeed, Sioux Indians often talk about the creator without much reference to Jesus or the Garden of Eden and say nothing about psychotherapy and theories of the collective unconscious in Western science terms. Spiritual traditions are not written about by legal scholars like Deloria with any degree of authenticity, let alone "translated" by editors who do not speak our language and are not tribal members. Let's not use this interest in philosophy to distract us from our own defense.

Well, you say, what about theory?

As we are told by C. R. Teuton in an essay called "Applying Oral Concepts to Written Traditions" in Jace Weaver's *Reasoning Together* (University of Oklahoma Press, 2008):

Theory is interdisciplinary—discourse with effects outside an original discipline.

Theory is analytical and speculative . . . an attempt to work out what is involved in what we call sex or language or writing or meaning or the subject.

Theory is a critique of common sense, of concepts taken as natural.

Theory is reflexive, thinking about thinking, enquiry into the categories we use in making sense of things, in literature and in other discursive practices. (67)

All of that comes, we are told, from the work of Jonathan Culler. And it is the material for any writing enterprise. Compelling! We love it! My prediction is that the book combining the musings of Deloria and Jung will find an eager audience in academe because it exemplifies the nature of theory. I am told that Vine wanted this manuscript published, and, according to some, he thought it was an essential part of his trilogy.

My silence on this matter means that I don't know what else to say. When my observations need an intellectual summation, I often fail to rise to the occasion. It is one of my flaws as a writer. Words often fail me. I will conclude by saying that this man was my intellectual and political hero, yes, a man of distinguished valor in the fields of law and politics though, admittedly, he was his Christian father's son. Father's legacies are often unfathomable in their continuing influence.

Christian leaders in the early 1800s, Vine's father among them, as representatives of the Almighty, were heads of enclaves given huge tracts of Indian treaty-protected land by the federal government (our "trustee") on every Indian reservation . . . not for themselves, but to build churches and start boarding schools so that the non-Christian indigenous populations could be converted and then governed in a colonial system right out of colonial America. It is a system in which some will say we are still, to this day, imprisoned.

We all have fathers who assist us in becoming. My Santee father, born just south of Old Agency at Sisseton, South Dakota, a man who never became a Christian, always thought this "giving" of land for churches was a brilliant political move on the part of the federal government because it, more than any other force, weakened the powerful Sioux Nation. This was always the aim of America. My father never thought giving land to churches was a religious or a moral move, nor did he think it was a philosophical move for the betterment of society. It was political. "Combining the Christian church and the U.S. government was a 'winner' for wasichus," he said, "indecent and criminal."

As an old rodeo rider who traveled throughout the West and even into Canada on the rodeo circuit, until he married my mother, who made him stop, my father gave little thought to philosophical matters. He knew Vine Deloria Sr., since they were of the same generation, and he said of Deloria, "He really knows how to use the English language." He said so *rather enviously*, I thought. Yet my father was a man who always preferred the old language of the Dakotas. When he and Vine Sr. talked together, they always "talked Indian."

My father's parents, Joe and Eliza, often went to the Christian convocations on the Yankton Sioux Reservation. Reverend Deloria was always a speaker there, and they knew him as a representative of the Episcopal Church. Their six sons, including my father, rarely accompanied them. What philosophy does, my father often said, is change the subject from "how can we steal your land and children," to "how can you get to heaven." It seemed to him, a cynic, to have been quite a successful strategy. I have found, too, that to change the subject has always been a winning tactic not only in scholarly and religious debates but in political ones too.

At the restaurant in Bellingham, I turned over in my hands the beautifully bound, sleekly covered book telling of Vine Jr.'s spirituality, and I pondered the notion of "the primitive" that is in the subtitle of the book. I ordered another gin and tonic (two is my limit) and told CJ. that I thought I'd change the subject of Vine's symposium from *spirituality and philosophy* to *politics and Indian studies*. I telephoned Vine's brother, Sam, who runs an Indian law center in New Mexico, and asked:

"Hey, Sam . . . in all your years, did you ever hear Vine talk at great length his own spirituality?"

"Hell, no!" he said, "but you know what, Liz. . . . Vine has always been a vessel into which people can put their own needs." He went on to say some complimentary things about Sioux brothers, and I added my own stuff about Sioux sisters because we both recognized the recent loss of parents and siblings and what a major bridge that is to cross.

The response I got from my inquiry gave me the courage to say what I had to say, which was that we should not, in our efforts to honor this man of letters, make him into something he was not. That often happens, as we all know, not only to scholars but to politicians and often to ordinary people. Remember your own Auntie Martha? A truly spiteful, mean, and selfish woman who drove her husband to drink and her children into silence? She is now, in memory, a talented quilt maker and "a revered elder" talked about in hushed tones at church gatherings as her family crumbles about her.

Truth is I had many conversations with Vine over the years, and they were always about politics and the law. We occasionally appeared on panels together, and never once did I hear him say anything at all about his own spirituality and not much, either, on religion as a moving force in his own personal life. Perhaps he knew of my disinterest in the subject.

To be sure, I did not know this man well, so some will think my remarks are unworthy of him. I do not know his wife nor his children. But the question of whether or not he should be remembered as a theologian and a leader in Native spiritual thinking rather than as one of the most important legal and political scholars of our time is something I take seriously. It's a big deal for me to try to get it right. I should say, reluctantly, that control of the public memory of a writer should probably not be left up to those who love him or her.

To say the important things about this man's work and the influence he has had on the thinking of Indians throughout the country is absolutely essential at gatherings like this symposium if we are to say what makes him the most significant political Indian thinker of the twentieth century. We should probably not waste our precious time on this earth talking about Vine's "spirituality," fascinating though it may be to those who say they are interested in the survival of the species, or piety itself.

The period of Vine's life (and mine) was particularly uneasy because the settler population in our part of the country still thought of Indians as originating in "primitivism" and "savagery" rather than in the sophisticated and practical notions of how to live on this earth without destroying it. The presence and history of indigenous peoples who walked this earth thousands of years before colonists came is not valued in today's fast-paced capitalist world.

What Vine's generation experienced was crucial to taking on the scholarly work and the real issues of the survival of Indian nationhood. It was a period when we "came close to the end," as Vine's very good friend Floyd "Red Crow" Westerman wrote in his songs. Neither of them were talking philosophy. They were talking politics and how to turn around mainstream white man's thinking vis-à-vis *the law*.

Vine took us through the darkest hours of the second half of the twentieth century, from 1950 when the assault on Native estates gave us little hope as indigenous peoples to the anti-Indian legislation against Native sovereignty of the 1980s and 1990s, which told us we would have to fight with everything we had to maintain our precarious survival as indigenous peoples and nations.

He interpreted for us the intent of the federal government as well as state governments in America and even the Christian churches in their historical roles as enemies of tribal interests. It was not a pretty sight. We took his textbooks into the classroom in an effort to inform ourselves and our students of the risks ahead. He changed, forever, the preposterous idea husbanded by colonial aggressors for five centuries that oppressed people would simply and easily give up their lives and their estates for the good of "others."

In spite of my undirected dinner conversation with my husband and in spite of the bewildered looks of my audience as I went into my rant on the importance of politics, the symposium was a grand success if its purpose was to bring people with a variety of diverse opinions together. Activists like Billy Frank, whom I hadn't seen in ten years, and the religious leaders of the Lummi Indians were all there acting as the convivial hosts. David Wilkins gave us the best of his scholarly and humorous and serious thinking, and we later shared coffee and the exquisite tribally prepared salmon. It is the kind of thing I engage in from time to time to remind myself that change can happen if one is patient enough to wait it out and aggressive enough to keep the eye on the prize, as they say.

When I got home I speculated some more on the beauty of the tribal estates of the Lummi and the loss of tribal estates throughout the country and the struggle to go on. The next morning I read in the local newspaper that the Badlands (part of the 1868 treaty lands) of the Sioux Nation might be "returned" to the Oglala and that there were "discussions" about how this could occur. I knew that Vine would surely have had some cryptic things to say about this recent development on the homelands.

These sovereign treaty lands were taken over in 1940 by the federal government and the U.S. military base here in Rapid City, Ellsworth Air Force Base. It was wartime, after all. And the lands were needed as a training base for the air force. Everyone had to sacrifice. The Sioux people who lived there were given two weeks to evacuate and have not been allowed to officially (and safely) return as landowners since.

That was in 1940? That's only eighty years ago! These things take time, don't you know.

In Indian Country, even when these ideas are recognized as the right thing to do or justified or moral, *these things take time.* Today, years later, the Oglalas (one band of the Seven Council Fires of the nation) are being told by the forest service in Pennington County, the U.S. bureaucracy that took over jurisdiction of the place when the air force left, that "conversations" could begin for the return of the Badlands.

How things have changed. Who we get to talk to about these matters arises from an *Alice in Wonderland* world called Sioux country. Being a cynic, I couldn't help but think of the time I heard Rosalie Little Thunder say some things about the so-called trust responsibility and her hope that we weren't "sitting at the wrong table again." It felt that way. "The point is," she said then, "the park service and the forest service in Pennington County has no authority to negotiate with the tribes." The purist that she was always came through for the people's wishes and desires.

But hey, let's try to be positive! It took only eighty years to get here! That's no time at all.

It took 354 years for the Catholic Church to decide that Galileo was right, after all, when he said the earth revolved around the sun. In 1633 the church condemned Galileo for saying correctly how the universe works, and the theologians held on to their fear and condemnation of this man and his beliefs and his science until 1992, when he was formally cleared of the crime of heresy.

These things take time.

When do we suppose the theft of the Sioux Nation estate in the Black Hills of what is now the state of South Dakota will be recognized as one of the crimes of human history and the land returned to its rightful owners? Will it be 345 years? Never? Tomorrow?

The return of the Badlands, history tells us, *will take time.*

12

I DISAPPOINT MYSELF THAT I cannot look at life without cynicism, cannot see the glass as half-full instead of half-empty. I am disappointed that I cannot be the poet I want to be, instead writing the political language of land and theft. Words, those sacred things that separate creators and artists like me from those who dance or make sensual sounds on the flute or paint or sculpt, deserve better than my morose contempt. Words, those sacred things that are not weightless to me, are too heavy to let my heart soar. They don't induce fictional dreams, nor do they help me convert my life into something more ethereal than blind alleys, cul-de-sacs with no exits. It's not like we can use paint or our beautiful bodies or musical instruments or eyes full of geographic wonder in photographs and electronics. Just words. That's all we chroniclers have to work with.

Writers like me, politically attuned always, put on our boots and slosh toward the future without wings, without the "cleansing with smoke" that my favorite poet, Ray Young Bear, speaks of in his poem "From the Landscape, A Superimposition" (*New Letters* 76, no. 4 [summer 2010]: 23). I admire him because he is like no other poet I know, a speaker of his tribal language who in English can superimpose — lay something on something else — to write the most eloquent poems of politics and culture. In contrast, my use of words, even when I am looking for that distant view that poetry requires, makes my work sound dull, pedantic, tedious, angry, and sad.

If I know that evergreen trees are never used in the Sun Dance of the Dakotapi because they are emblems of mourning, I ought to know that words, told to us by the cottonwoods my Santee kunshi knew of, offer life and joy and eventual rain to cleanse the prairie grass. The dances and the songs of the Sioux are *not* dances and songs of mourning. They are expressions of joy and life and survival and strength!

This suggests that I would like to use the words of a poet or symbolist because I have confidence in the future. Yet as a political writer rather than a poet or a devotee of some practical piety or a dancer, I apparently can't move on. I'm done for. Reclaiming an ugly history. Letting sagacious words of policy do all the work that words appealing to ideal beauty should and could do.

In my notes, instead of suggesting that visiting the permanent metaphysical nature of life in this universe would be a way forward, I say this:

if it was easy for the Congress to pass the Allotment Act (1887),
specifically the Dawes Severalty Act
which diminished the Indian Tribal Economic Base
by 140 million acres to approximately 50 million
acres in 40 years (with more loss to come),
why isn't it just as easy for Congress to give it back?

When your notes and words start there, you can go on with instance after instance. In 1904 Teddy Roosevelt, right here within driving distance of where I live, issued a proclamation opening up four hundred thousand acres of Indian land for "settlement," as though it was not already "settled."

I can't seem to move on. I am done for.

The truth is I don't like being referred to as a poet because, even though I would rather write poetry than do anything except eat at Chinese restaurants with my grandchildren, that label is wholly dishonest. I know I haven't fallen in love with language in the same way that others have, sensually, obsessively.

95

Returning to Jung and Vine Deloria, let me say this: if, after I bite the dust, anyone reads my few poems and says, "wasn't she a spiritual person?," I will have to come back from the dead to haunt whoever that overweening gasbag is—probably some professor of literature in some obscure English department.

When I applied for a visa several years ago, I was tempted to put "writer" on the line asking for my occupation. Instead, I put "professor." My friend, who also was applying for a visa for the first time, said she put "poet" on the dotted line when she went to England on sabbatical. She was thrilled at her own audacity, not having published a complete book of poems yet, only those lone pieces that appear in dark, dim, abstruse little magazines read by no one except other obscure poets.

As it turned out, it didn't really matter because she eventually did publish a collection of poems and hopes to go on to greater things. As for me, truthfully, I've still never been anywhere in the universe except the other nations on this continent, Mexico and Canada.

My friend and I thought about going to Italy. "Do I really want to go to Italy?" the long-haired beauty from Oakland asked. "Do I really want to see the statues of Orpheus and Eurydice in Naples? If so, why?"

I had no answer.

With my usual churlishness I suggested, "Maybe you'd rather see the house where Dante wrote *The Inferno*, a house covered now, I'm sure, with moss and dust and insects busily gnawing at its roots."

More silence.

"Maybe I'd like to see the Pope?" she ventured.

"Yeah? What did he write?"

She raised her eyebrows and laughed out loud. We both knew we would never go to Italy together.

The truth is, I told her, instead of going to Italy, I'd rather dance with my daughters at Crown Butte, smell the vapors of my buckskin, and listen to my beads and shells accompanying the drum as I walk across the heavy grass toward the arbor. What free time I have had over the years has sometimes been spent doing just that. At other times I've hung out with other obscure (and sometimes not so obscure) writers. The only times I've encountered real or famous or notorious writers usually happened quite randomly.

Once, when I accompanied my first husband, Melvin Paul Traversie Cook, to the Mayo Clinic in Rochester, Minnesota (where he was diagnosed with the diabetes that eventually killed him long after I'd left him) we encountered a panic-stricken Ernest Hemingway. We were walking in an underground hallway filled with patients going from one lab to the next. Hemingway was in a wheelchair being pushed by a serene and clear-eyed middle-aged nurse, hardly five feet tall, who treated him as though he were a recalcitrant child who was refusing to sit on mommy's lap in the midst of rushing traffic.

His white, straggly hair stood on end, and he was using every cuss word he knew, bellowing at her that she was a "whore" and a "cunt," waving his beefy white arms that were covered with black hair, and lurching forward in an animal crouch as though ready to pounce.

"There goes the old man," Mel quipped as we stepped aside, "in a sea of bad words and panic, shittin' in his own nest!"

Mixed metaphor or not, Mel was a man of words too. It was one of the things that had attracted me to him years before, just after he got back from Korea.

Two weeks later we read in the newspaper that the old man had gone to Ketchum, Idaho, where he blew his brains out. I began to wonder then what a writer's retreat with Hemingway would have been like. How perverse is that!

One of the best times hanging out with writers was in 2006 when I was invited to the Island Institute in Sitka, Alaska, a writer's group founded nearly twenty years before in an area where a sense of place is the major theme. I know this is not as exciting as the presence of Hemingway would have been, nor would it have been as cool as if we were to join what's left of the Beats in San Francisco, but for me it was a wonderful respite from the usual hullaballoo and cloying earnestness of writers' gatherings. The literary focus was landscape and community, and I was invited at the behest of a novelist friend, John Keeble, who lives in rural Washington State, where he writes stunning stories and novels reflecting those concerns.

Before I left for Sitka, I stopped at Elliot Bay Co., a bookstore in Seattle, and gave a reading of fiction that was attended by four people, one of whom was my long-suffering husband, CJ. When I told John about this humiliating episode, he said, "Join the club, Liz. I read there from my book *Out of the Channel*" — his description of the Alaska oil spill of 1989 — "and the only person who came was my son! I think he came because he lives there, but they do have great coffee!" He smiled.

Wouldn't you have thought that such a book about the oil spill would have been of red-hot interest to the people of Puget Sound, since just north of there lie the fabulous oil fields that will continue to be raped by careless capitalists from around the world? Well, so much for landscape and community in the city of Seattle.

It was such a relief to get to Sitka and the workshop, where there has been an effort to cultivate uncommon conversations about the nature of our connections as human beings to the greater natural world. This was before the rise of Sarah Palin and her story of a woman filled with massive confidence based in massive ignorance, who has changed all political subjects to "mama grizzlies" and "tea parties."

The 2006 Sitka symposium brought together a faculty of Muslim, Buddhist, Native American, Middle Eastern, and varied Western perspectives to talk about how to shape a different world. There were about fifty participants. Out of this experience and many others, I have concluded in my old age that the great notion most American writers often start with (that it is all about me, me, me) needs revision.

Sandy Tolan, the author of *The Lemon Tree: An Arab, A Jew, and the Heart of the Middle East*, was there. So was Micheline Marcom, born in Saudi Arabia and raised in Los Angeles, to talk of *Three Apples Fell from Heaven*, dealing with the Armenian genocide. Alan Senauke, a Soto Zen Priest from Berkeley, and Rabia Harris from Nyack, New York, both speak about reconciliation and write passionately about structural violence and issues of international peace. Lots of people from the non-Native communities were there to tell stories and to enjoy the extracurricular activities that ranged from a cruise on the sound to drinking beer, schnapps, and whatever else with the fishermen at the wharf who went out early and stayed late.

It occurred to me that I could go to the tourist shops and buy a bikini made of moose hide and fur, but frankly, even in my reckless youthful days I would never have imagined seeing such sexy duds along with the accompanying woolen penis covers displayed in the windows to attract tourists. The contrasts in places like Sitka, now overtaken by North American capitalists, are jarring. We met a man named Jerry who invited us to his place and cooked fresh salmon for us. About two weeks later, a package arrived for me in Rapid City, sent by Jerry. It was some of the most wonderful salmon preserved in the traditional way!

Speaking of traditions, during my visit in Sitka, a couple of Native Inuit women, a mother and daughter, sought me out and invited me to a clan peace hat ceremony conducted in their Native language. Afterward, they told me how the Russians came and destroyed most of their clan houses on the coastal range and later the U.S. Navy came and destroyed some more. Now, they said, they have only four clan houses left, but they are survivors, and they still possess language and customs. When I couldn't attend the great feast they were having, they later brought me a huge platter of food, much of it from the sea.

I found it interesting that there is, in the middle of the city, a huge Russian (Lutheran?) church that rises above the streets, and a few blocks away a massive retirement home that houses several dozen Russian retired persons among lush gardens of roses and ferns and vines. It is the one edifice to a historical past that probably should be burned to the ground, but is further evidence that murderous colonials and imperial militaries never do go away completely, nor do their self-serving histories.

More significantly, it is evidence of the forgiving nature of the indigenes, who can't and won't carry around the baggage and burdens of their own vicious colonial history that no one else can bear to acknowledge. How does one talk of shaping a different world if one provides the perpetrators with old-age comfort but does not call them to the courts of law as criminals who deserve punishment?

I did not express these unkind thoughts mostly because I was enthralled with the sense of place in Sitka that is simply too overwhelming to be free of until you get on your plane and leave. The feeling of thrall doesn't last long. When you leave, unfortunately, you return to your old morose self. I also did not speak up because in the collaborative problem-solving sessions, we talked about affordable housing and long-term solid waste plans, even as I wanted to think more about the crimes of coloniality and postcoloniality, the subject matter so obvious in Sitka and also the subject of a new book I was starting to shape.

There was a marvelous bookstore on the main drag, and I hung out there a lot. The adjoining coffee and sandwich shop was a place where you could sit and start a conversation with people who had come to Alaska from other places in the United States and had stayed on to develop a camaraderie as moving as anything I've ever experienced.

These were people who were taking over these indigenous lands so rich and compelling. They were never going home again, and you had to have in your heart some compassion for both the Inuit peoples I met who told me of their displacement and the newcomers who so desperately wanted to call this place home. Even their old and wrinkled Russian forebears, still hanging on to their stolen colonial possessions, seemed pitiful and worthy of kindness. I've never said that about the Germans and Swedes who overtook Sioux country.

As for the writing retreat, my interests seemed just too far out of the mainstream of that little group, many of whom were interested in the business of developing communities and getting on with tourist planning. Their day-to-day workshops reflected those interests — stuff that is really not my thing. If I wanted to do economic development, I could go home to the Fort, where such help is badly needed. Frankly, I have so few real skills that are useful to such places.

Instead, I tend to continue my talks and my writings about unattended historical crimes in communities like Sitka, where Indians once were in charge but are now displaced by settlers. The crimes that have been suffered by indigenous peoples all over the globe are usually unmentioned in such gatherings attended by American writers, but they bleed into a future giving us constant war and violence and ubiquitous poverty in a country filled with toys and conveniences for the richest people on the planet. These criminal matters are still the critical thrust of my writing. I will always be grateful, though, for my Sitka sojourn. This kind of community writers' group, which lasted only a week, is so badly needed in communities where I live because such groups do make us try to pay attention to each other and force us to come face to face with the views of others who have their own perspectives.

Two years after my Sitka experience, which brought to light how lush an isolated environment is and how it needs our care, Greenpeace came to the Black Hills and visited the most famous tourist place of them all, about twenty miles from our house, the faces on Mount Rushmore. The people, called Greeners by the locals, were treated as a body of criminals trespassing on the "sacred ground" of Mount Rushmore, which actually resides here as a fake tourist mecca that makes a mockery of the indigenous presence. I was shaken by the obvious absurdity of the effort yet touched by the moral perspective brought to it.

That morning I had turned on the television not really intending to watch but to break the silence of the day and saw a photo of a sign hanging for a few moments on the presidential heads on the Rushmore monument. It said, "Stop global warming," put there, we were told by the newscaster, by Greenpeace activists. As you probably know, Greenpeace is the world's most effective environmental activist group in the country and around the world, dedicated to understanding climate change and saving forests and oceans.

From the point of view of Lakota/Dakota activists I know, the historical landlords in the region, the Greenpeacers, I thought, were a little late, but as is often said, *better late than never*. A few days after their gallant effort, we heard that the organization was fined thirty thousand dollars in the U.S. federal courts and the South Dakota legal establishment for the criminal act of "trespassing on government property." Whose property? In 1980 the Supreme Court of the United States said this property was stolen from the Sioux Nation by the U.S Congress, an edict that fell quickly into silence, and the theft remains one of the historical crimes of human history.

"Government property" is a big deal around here. Even the reservations (supposedly treaty-protected estates of the Sioux Nation) are sometimes thought to be "government property," held "in trust" by colonial law. Once, when a young Indian man brought a trespassing case against the Bureau of Indian Affairs for its personnel coming on to his land without his permission, he was told by the federal court in this region, "The Bureau personnel can go anywhere on Indian land. They do not need your permission. They are not trespassers."

The whole fiasco of the Greenpeace intrusion brought up the question I've had all my life: what is the appropriate function of the law in a democratic world? To steal land from Indians and claim ownership? To make criminals of environmental activists who want to make a public statement but who do not destroy or steal property or endanger the citizenry? None of it seems appropriate as an example of legal enlightenment.

As a Dakota Sioux with a historical and spiritual tribal connection to the hills and as one who has followed the criminal act of theft of lands in this place that has happened over the centuries, I found it particularly ironic that the rule of law, which in 1877 said it was okay to steal 7.7 million acres of land from Indians protected by treaty, now says that ordinary citizens must be criminalized if they "trespass" on this very same stolen land.

Does anyone get irony anymore?

When Kierkegaard described irony, he talked about how the ironist was a woman who sucked the blood out of her lover and then fanned him with coolness as though she would let him live. How she lulled him to sleep and then tormented him by not letting him sleep because she gave him nightmares. I am not sure about the malice that great philosopher speaks of in his definition, especially since his perpetrator is a woman, but the expected virtue of the law continues to be smeared by a variety of inexplicable interpretations. The rule of law of these United States has allowed people to blow up and devastate an entire sacred mountain geography so that the sculptures of "democratic" and "humane" leaders like Lincoln and Washington could lead and dedicate a nation claiming to understand the sacredness of this place for the last few centuries. To suggest that any of these settler-people and their agents have tried to even tangentially understand the sacredness of the place while periodically dynamiting nature's treasures would seem almost comical to me if it weren't so sad.

There was probably a teachable moment in the whole fracas, but no one in the community has ever taken such occasions up as a cause. Even Indians fall silent on the matter. For us it seems that it does no good to challenge people to "listen up" about the devastation of our planet if the "art" we sculpt on mountains destroys the meaning and relationship of the earth to us as humans. It is even less realistic if we are to know anything about our concomitant relationship with each other as treaty participants.

The final irony was the choice of the Rushmore monument for the Greenpeace demonstration which unwittingly said publicly, "America honors its leaders." Revering without question the images of presidents whose policies were imperialistic in order to legitimize land theft from indigenous peoples is unconscionable. The Shrine of Democracy is the name given to this effort that has resulted in the domination of a colonized "protectorate" toward indigenous peoples.

Probably there are no art forms that are not political.

I think it was a cadre of anthropologists who a hundred years ago believed they had created a discipline that could be called non-ideological, a scholarship of apolitical, detached objectivity and a commitment to scientific methodology. These academic types have now spent a hundred years collecting the spoils of colonial conquest, calling it "discovery" and "exploration" and hoping for the best. They have created an academic mythology much the same way that writers create personal mythologies when we write memoirs and biographies. No one is blameless.

The effort to place a Native perspective even in the most benign of circumstances in the rubble of the historical narrative in Sioux country seems to me almost futile. The Crazy Horse Memorial adjoining the Rushmore faces (which requires more celebratory TNT blasts into the sacred hills every year), is a monstrous insult to the Indians who have lived here for millennia for lots of reasons, but surely because no one except the arrogant white immigrant sculptor (now deceased) even knows what the Indian leader looked like. It is more than just local lore that Crazy Horse wouldn't allow himself to be photographed. It is a historical fact that there are *no photographs* of this man in existence.

To put an image in the white sculptor's imagination on a devastated mountain is beyond historical obscenity. It should be a crime, but it seems only white men and the gods know how to define crime. Larry McMurtry, the popular chronicler of all things Indian and Western, even wrote a book with what he suggested might be a Crazy Horse picture on the cover. The arrogance of these incidents by artists is indecent, but, then, a lot of art is indecent.

In the following year, as further evidence of the limits of how the white settlers that surround Sioux country are not the embodiment of humanity they claim to be, a young Oglala Indian student, a relative of Crazy Horse, was refused a request he made to his U.S. government to wear his tribal regalia at his high school graduation in a little town south of the Shrine of Democracy.

· When he took his request to court, saying it was his right to honor his achievement in his tribal way, he was told by an all-white school board that granting his request would "invite abuse" and "undermine" a formal occasion. The courts agreed. This kind of not-so-subtle irony is lost to most observers, and many of us feel a little ridiculous trying to make the point that we really do have our own roles to play in reenactments.

If you are an Indian trying to use your own history to describe your present condition, your words are often said to "invite criticism" from the broader non-Indian community. An editor at a local newspaper once told me that he could not publish my submission because "your last letter to the editor was criticized by several readers regarding its angry tone, and we are hoping to avoid that since it only tends to draw the racists out of the closet." This is said with a straight face even though the Rush Limbaugh radio show, which spouts hate for hours each day, is the most popular radio show in the region. The editor told me about my angry tone even as he was trying not to reject my latest commentary. As an inveterate and outspoken letter-writer whose opinions and thoughts are often out of the mainstream, such rebukes seem petty to me.

The only other previous Indian letter-writer uncowed by rejection and vilification in this part of the country was a woman known to my parents' generation. I didn't know her except by reputation. She was the mother of the famed Sioux defense attorney Ramon Roubideaux, and she lived in the hills for most of her adult life. One of her relatives told me she wrote a letter to the editor even on the day she died.

The kind of censorship I'm talking about here, while it just seems silly to me, is really a most injurious kind of violence in any community because it robs all of the citizens of the process of learning from one another. The local newspaper tells me, "if we print your comments, we have to print the replies, and I and my editors find that counterproductive."

I'm not sure we should all agree with that position.

Ever since the Restoration printing days decades ago, a literate public set guidelines for a civil discourse, and they seemed reasonable enough then, to be sure. As early as 1710 copyright laws came into being, and further order amounting to censorship was imposed by those in power. So now we have to ask: how did we get to Rush Limbaugh? The principles of civil discourse and freedom of the press are among the contemporary ideas that are being encouraged or discouraged according to whim in the name of democracy in this city and elsewhere. Today with the internet in full force, there is no privacy, no secrets, and in the end, no sense of shame.

In a recent letter to the local editor, I tried to say something publicly about how the sacred Black Hills area is now being destroyed and threatened by oil developers, and I gave it the title of "Environmentalists and Indians Lose Again." I stated the position of the state to allow oil drilling close to a sacred site. I quoted a Santee Dakota historical figure named Little Crow because he, too, had something to say about the invasion of capitalists into his territory, and his words were recorded in various venues over a hundred years ago.

I was told rather reluctantly by the sympathetic editor that yes, the newspaper would publish my letter on the op-ed page, but having seen some of my earlier work, she couldn't resist giving me a lecture about how to best "get ideas across." She even suggested that I write a longer piece—a "guest-edited" explanation would, perhaps, be more reliable—but I declined.

What I had thought I was doing in writing a letter to the editor, as a good citizen of the community should do now and then, was protesting the news that the drilling for oil one mile from the sacred site called in English Bear Butte was about to begin, and I found it offensive and thought other people might agree.

The editor, it seemed, was not so certain of my intentions.

13

THE GIST OF THIS episode illustrates the notion that history and the environment, sense of place and myth, and the effort to share the broader meaning of culture and experience is a complicated business.

The name of a significant butte in the newspaper article, often called Mato Tipila or the Bear's Home by Indians (a reference to their ancient knowledge of the stars), implies that it is known to the Ocheti Sakowan as a place of origin of the people.

What I wrote to the newspaper was fairly straightforward:

The State of South Dakota has just approved the drilling in a thousand acre oil field a mile from the sacred site called Bear Butte in spite of the heroic efforts of some in this community to stop the desecration. We are told no opponents appeared at the hearing. If that is true it means people here have made their uneasy and futile peace with the continuing greed and racism that surrounds this site. In 1862, the charismatic chieftain of the Santee Dakotahs, Little Crow, told as much to those who witnessed the theft of his treaty-protected homeland. He said, "The white people are locusts. They are as thick as tamaracks in the swamps of the Ojibway. They fall on the trees and devour the leaves in one day." The Board of Minerals and Environments, like the locusts Little Crow spoke of, will desecrate the environment of the Mato Sapa for 4 million barrels of oil; when that is exhausted they will fly like locusts to the next forest and oil field. It is unrealistic for us to expect that anything we do will stop them.

I thought the quote was a fine and grave metaphor used by a chief who was leading his people to defend themselves in war against the invaders who today say they own the "private" land, and besides, as a woman who loves the experiment with words that comes with being a writer, I thought it demonstrated the gracefulness of our tribal language, even in translation.

The news editor, who said nothing about the literary skill of the powerful speaker of an old language, nonetheless admitted that she was shocked and appalled when she first read about the drilling project because she had hiked near the butte and she loved to do so, but she said I should be careful about what I write in letters to the editor. She said it in this way, "I know that if you cross the line into name calling, rather than what Bear Butte means to Native Americans, and its history, editors here will not allow it. We have pretty rigid policies about not allowing angry or uncivil discourse or inflaming racism or reverse racism."

"This means," she went on, "it would require some *semantic adjustments* and *extreme diplomacy* to get your points across. I guess what I am trying to say is that an angry rant won't be allowed, even though I fully understand your anger." She mentioned again that "semantic adjustments" might be needed and that I should use "extreme diplomacy" to "get points across." Diplomacy. Tact.

My letter, it had seemed to me when I wrote it, was a model of reasonableness. I told her that my letter was based in our history, hers and mine. After some consideration she allowed it to be printed in the paper.

As I later examined the meaning of this episode, I came to the conclusion that the words of Little Crow, who led the war against the illegal white settlers in Minnesota, would be wiped from history in 2010 just as the Santee Reservation was wiped from the face of the state of Minnesota in 1863 if this editor was to prevail. To use Little Crow's historical words in modern discourse was unacceptable after 147 years because they might "incite" readers. The fragile nature of our present lives was to be edited for reasons that seemed like unnecessary censorship.

As a spokesperson for our history in this country, Little Crow was to be silenced by, of all things, a third-rate local publication called a newspaper. We know that, yes, someone did incite the war he led. The consequences of that brief war were dire for everyone who survived it. But it was very likely not the speaker of the apt metaphor who was forced into leading the defensive stance he took. It was more probably the thieves who aggressively claimed thousands of acres of his homelands and continue to claim them by forcing his people into poverty and starvation.

Such modern-day incidents fit rather well in understanding the ongoing principles not only of news writing but of historiography in America concerning its settlement and its dealings with the people of the First Nations of this country. What it means is that it is not "productive," as the editor says, to violate those principles of historical colonization even though the expressions are advocated by many non-Indian community members.

What does this demonstrate about how history is manipulated? Is there a name for that? Is a newspaper a system for preaching a gospel, or is it an organ of information, facts, and data through which its readers can reach rational solutions to their questions? The debates over how to shape civic and "civil" dialogue have always been endangered by restricting the flow of information, and it happens even in this cyberspace age. Why not call it propaganda? Are these editors proselytizers? Many of the earliest colonizers used their power to establish their authority, yet their mission as the first historians should seem to be sacrosanct.

The desire to maintain the American myth of freedom and democratic values of inclusiveness and diversity is threatened by Little Crow's history, even in the face of the concern by everyday people evident at every level of society. Yet the local newspaper is still, for me at least, a weather vane for public discourse and information despite its limitations. We should probably not let its discourse go uncommented upon.

These incidents are not isolated. They happen frequently all over the country. It's an old story in America.

And when this kind of resistance to real history is so carefully managed into tiresome self-interest by those who are in charge, it fosters silence or despair. Many publications in our region that call themselves newspapers have a front page, four pages of sports, three pages of news from the Christian churches, and then eight pages of the classifieds. Agreed, it's not the *New York Times*, but shouldn't we expect something more relevant to the diverse lives that many people actually live?

What I fail to admit to myself is that just because Bob Woodward and Carl Bernstein brought down a corrupt regime in our time, such journalistic works are anomalies, not marvels of everyday news discourse in everyday communities. My speaking of it here is not some kind of tedious self-pity from an author whose work has often been thought to be polemical and marginal and even hateful. It is, instead, an examination of why American Indian writers like myself continue to be much more politically engaged than most mainstreamers, even though there is often nowhere to turn.

It is not enough for poets and writers to keep repeating that the warlords in Somalia and the people who fought against the Sandinista revolution were dictators. We know that. What we are not allowed to say is that the presidencies of the United States have also been at times filled with warlords and dictators that caused the deaths of millions on this continent and that saving babies and airlifting food to the victims will probably not do it. The need for a reliable political discourse is crucial.

Fig. 1. Author, 1975. From the author's collection.

Fig. 2. Author and grandson, 1982. From the author's collection.

Fig. 3. Author, 2008. Photo courtesy Joe Collins. From the author's collection.

Fig. 4. Author and late husband, 2013. Photo courtesy of Mary A. Cook.
From the author's collection.

Fig. 5. Author in traditional dress, 2016. Photo courtesy of Mary A. Cook. From the author's collection.

14

WE NATIVE WRITERS ARE told, always, that even though we are
angry about historical realities, we must write out of the need to
escape from ourselves and fulfill social responsibilities to the country, to democracy, to our treasured legacies, to Christian thankful-
ness and generosity. Many Native artists have tried to do this. Many
Native politicians have tried to do this. They are, in my view, the
sad cases that do not admit to the hatred the indigene feels toward
invaders and colonists and imperialists who have taken over the land
and made them beggars.

To write or to create art without acknowledging that hate borne
of historical experience is a genuine thing is to, one way or another,
abandon political matters, forget the tremendous pressures of tribal
histories in this country, and move on into metaphysics, fantasy,
cyberspace, or other opportunistic attitudes that will get the writer
or researcher or professor tenure, three cars in the garage, and a
lifetime academic chair in sociology or law. Better yet, a seat at the
tribal council table.

Saying that it is okay to be expressing the reality of hatred in given
expressions of historical storytelling, which I often do, is not to suggest that one should use one's energy to write about how you hate
your first wife or your teachers or the kid who wouldn't give you the
swing at recess time during your schooldays or the husband who got
drunk and beat you up. I am talking about responding to real issues
of Indian reaction to historical experience about which there has
been so little defense and commitment.

One Native writer who cannot keep herself from answering the social and political call for commitment to realism is Waziyatawin (Angela Cavender Wilson), who possesses a PhD in history from Cornell and who also uses the words of the charismatic chieftain of the Santee, Little Crow, in many of her dissertations. She has made the charge that white occupants of Minnesota participated in the historical reality of genocide and still do.

In November 2010 she went to Winona State University in Winona, Minnesota, and gave a talk on her book *In the Footsteps of Our Ancestors*. She made the point that the mass hanging of thirty-eight Santees after the Little Crow War in 1862 and the theft of the Santee homelands a year later left blood on the hands of all Minnesotans, then and now. At one point, she told her audience, the Dakotas possessed 54,017,532 acres of land, and they knew how to live. Today they possess seven thousand acres of land, hardly enough to run a decent-sized cattle ranch in the Midwest. She said that Indian scalps were worth two hundred dollars in the days that followed, which I have known to be true at the time of my parents' generation on the Crow Creek Sioux Reservation, where I grew up. It was only after that generation that the high wooden fence boundaries to protect white settlers on Indian lands around the agency were taken down, and the killing of Indians in that way stopped. Wilson tells her audience that this is not ancient history, that it is in the actual experience of our relatives and in the memory of all of us who are Isianti.

She has said, as many have, that this was ethnic cleansing, crimes not unknown or lost to history, and that America must own up to its own actions. Santees like Wilson know this history, but when they tell it to the ancestors of the white perpetrators of these atrocities, they are vilified and told to write with diplomacy and tact. Such reminders anger many Americans, especially those in the Midwest, who have an embarrassingly failed background of their own historical legacies.

One white student listener in the Winona audience became incensed during Dr. Wilson's presentation and, feeling threatened, wrote in the local newspaper, "This intimidation presented by this accredited author was not only inappropriate but also criminal. The First Amendment only guarantees freedom of speech when it is not littered with imminent threat." His feelings of his perceived victimization were absurd if not simple-minded, but they were credible enough in that part of the country to get the attention of the FBI, who ran a quick investigation of Dr. Wilson.

"Like all our Dakota warriors in 1862," Wilson had said, "Little Crow was full of anger and rage, and he had no qualms about using any means necessary to fight for Dakota liberation." It was the "any means necessary" that brought about the student's objection. When that same phrase was used by President George W. Bush in 2004 to capture and kill his enemy Saddam Hussein, America applauded. There has been little protest of this kind of language when colonists have wanted to defend themselves. But for an American Indian like Wilson to say such a thing, it becomes a criminal act, one severe enough to be investigated by the police.

War is the initiator of such talk and such actions, and the fact that Minnesotans and their scholarly historians have called the Little Crow War a "conflict" or an "uprising" for the last hundred years instead of a declared war is reflected in this student's pathetic ignorance. It is not his fault that he believes his people did not commit war crimes nor that he is ignorant of a war declared by Little Crow in what is now called the state of Minnesota. It is not this student's fault that he knows so little of the Santee people who fought courageously against white immigrant occupiers and stealers of their lands. Education on these matters in Minnesota and elsewhere is totally inadequate to the challenge, if not a reflection of racial bias.

Wilson, as a Dakota scholar, was expressing the rage we all have. She does not need to tell her own people about the trait that connects herself as a writer-teacher to Little Crow, the man who went to war to defend his people. That trait, known by all Santees, is this: he was a compelling orator and patriot. She, a compelling writer, joins that history in which neither of them have had reason to succumb to censorship by authorities or by uninformed students.

Her charge that today's Minnesotans have a responsibility to claim their own history of massacre and death and theft that is the legacy of the Dakota Tribe in that state is long overdue. As evidence that a few Indians are also ignorant of their own history, we find out in the few days after her presentation that she was immediately set upon by elected Santee tribal leaders Roger Trudell, Wilfred Keeble, Mike Selvage, and Tony Reider, who said they spoke for the people who, they said, rejected her charges against the Minnesota community. The headline was "Sioux Nation Rejects Author's Statements." Some suggest that these bureaucrats are elected to do the bidding of the federal government, and they seldom speak accurately for the people on all occasions.

The saddest thing of all in the Wilson case is the extent to which these colonial leaders and entities such as federally funded tribal councils, community alliances for unity, and collaborators at all levels of reservation and urban Indian populations lead public attacks on Dr. Wilson's words and intellectual leadership. Some people who do that receive massive patronage from the church, the colonials, the bureaucrats, and governments that run their lives. They are the same traitors and appeasers who led to the subjugation of the Dakotas in the 1860s and, worse, to the untimely death of Taoyateduta who knew, as Wilson knows, that he had detractors who were fools and cowards.

For many years following these events, Dr. Wilson did not teach in her homelands. Like many thinkers on this continent who choose to fight off colonial regimes and live outside of the countries of their origin, she spends much of her intellectual time outside of Dakota country. She joins Carlos Fuentes, Pablo Neruda, Alfonso Reyes, Wole Soyinka, Octavio Paz, and countless other writers have often been exiled, often threatened and vilified.

When I was growing up on the Isianti-Hunkapi-Ihanktowan reservation called Crow Creek, I didn't read daily newspapers, not even a weekly, living out there in the middle of beautiful grasslands and creeks, listening to the meadowlarks singing songs of courage in a dangerous world. We subscribed to almost nothing in the way of news publications. But we knew our own history and treasured it in the stories we were told by our elders. We knew, too, that it was a history of violence.

The overwhelming question today, then, is why many of us continue on this course when we recognize that we are victims of the corrupt American myth and are increasingly sure that most of what we say or write is destined to be chewed up and spit out by people who want to remake history. Some victims become "part-time Indians," and even then they sometimes find their work ousted from the curriculum. What must scholars who appreciate Wilson's work do? How can we defend her position that is based in a history so ugly that no one, not even the victims, can utter its truth? There are no easy answers to that question.

I've been a news writer and even an editor, so I understand the public and bureaucratic impulse to control what is said and what is written. My understanding may be one of the reasons for this eccentric and unexpected sojourn into writing a memoir so late in my life. As I've sat at my desk to write, I've asked, *should I use this occasion to vent my anger?* I have plenty of it. Editors and publishers and even readers are ever present, so the chances that I might get away with it are slim.

Should I become an insurrectionist and refuse to pay my taxes? That, too, involves scrutiny and risk. Should I become a pacifist and say it is okay to steal land and kill Indians and pass laws that diminish home rule and saddle us with gambling casinos for "economic development"? These are choices and decisions to consider.

15

THE ULTIMATE QUESTION FOR me as I begin to respond to various writing and teaching and research options is *what is the function of history, or more specifically in this case, the "memoir"?*

There are no quick answers. Maybe I should try to become Ernesto Cardenal, who saw the revolution in his country (Nicaragua) as a "fragment of cosmic liberation," which he says is a form of love. So, like Cardenal, perhaps I should become a real poet and devote my work to those ends.

In the end it is, after all, not about me or you; it is not personal, nor has it ever been. Writing a memoir is not for the purpose of shaking the family tree to either condemn or commemorate those who gave me life or those who disagree with me. It is not about transcending the early flaws of those who may or may not have done the right thing in my childhood, which seems to be the twentieth-century rationale for memoir writing. It is not to vent years of anger and indecision and regret. Its main purpose is not to blame a warped adult life, if that is how we end up, on someone other than ourselves. It's not about revenge, nor is it even an effort to try to figure out what happened and why, though that might be revealing.

Reading the works available in the genre are helpful. As I was writing this, George W. Bush published *Decision Points* (Random House, 2010), his perspective about his presidency. It was later described as "George Bush, an Unexamined Life," by some insightful but snotty reviewer in one of the slick magazines I sometimes read. I love those bad reviews of bad books, even though the poet

W. H. Auden once said to engage in writing nasty notices for books was bad for the character of all participants. Such a moralist! Bush's biography is simply the narrative of a third-string high school jock and upwardly mobile Yale cheerleader who became president of the strangest democracy of our time, a story that became a cruel joke and is useful only for making excuses that unwittingly reveal to his readers his blatant white-man privileged status. Maybe his painting of portraits will fare better.

The truth is, history, if history in memoir writing is any judge, cannot tell us who is right and who is wrong. Dubya's intention was clear: focusing on how to make decisions, he wants his readers to know that it is pretty easy to make even monumental decisions like going to war with falsified information and waterboarding your captives, even getting your troops to murder the leader of a sovereign country and his sons, if, and his is a big *if*, he says, "you know who you are and what your values are."

So that is the grand purpose: an examination of your values? How many times have we heard that mantra? Do you have to make excuses for yourself in order to write a memoir? Of course! Dubya says he wants his memoir to "serve as a resource for those who study history." Well, that's another explanation for writing a memoir. It has become an accepted practice for our presidents to build monuments to themselves and write books about what they remember of their tenures. We must not expect that they will denounce themselves.

I recently read a memoir by the very popular novelist Annie Proulx, who sits gazing at the North Platte River and the eagles near her Medicine Bow Ranch in Wyoming. She tells us "these eagles have been calm and laid-back . . . wonderful parents with a high success rate." They have raised two chicks every year except one, she says, and when a stranger is seen, they fly over scrutinizing them carefully. Does one have to become an anthropologist while writing a memoir? Maybe not, but you surely want to be careful about repeating yourself before you become a chicken!

That hadn't occurred to me until I read a review in the *New York Times*, which ran a little squib on *You Don't Have to Say You Love Me* (Little, Brown, 2017), by the Native American writer Sherman Alexie, asking how to handle repetition, which I am told is a trait in many, many memoirs. The *Times* critic tells us that the poet repeats the word "loss" thirteen times, thus, "My name is Sherman Alexie and I was born from loss and loss and loss and loss and loss and loss and . . ." Well, you get the point, don't you? The critic makes this point in his evaluation, "Everyone knows the childhood game of saying a familiar word so many times that it becomes alien, and that's what happens here: by the thirteenth iteration, 'loss' feels less like a word than like a sort of mouth-stone, strange and round, burbling out of your open face over and over and over again, like eggs out of a relentless chicken." What? What?

Leslie Marmon Silko in the beautifully written work called *The Turquoise Ledge* (Viking, 2010) tells us she rescues rattlesnakes from parrot wire in her yard and that her special snake, Evo, an indoor rattlesnake, is edgy after she gets back from Mexico, and she has to wait until he molts before he will eat what she offers him. Should one become a herpetologist to write a memoir of the desert life?

It is my view that Silko could be compared in subsequent reviews to Loren Eiseley, the naturalist who wrote a favorite of mine, *The Immense Journey* (Time, 1946). Though he is a bit more scientific than Silko, he is not more imaginative. Silko seeks out the turquoise stone on her daily walks in the desert, which she describes as her relentless quest to expose what is happening in the modern world to her Eden.

Russell Means, the charismatic Lakota leader of the American Indian Movement, wrote *Where White Men Fear to Tread* (St. Martin's, 1984), saying his mother was an "abusive" parent who beat him and treated him badly, a self-serving statement accepted as true by subsequent biographers. Do you have to become contemptuous of your elders while writing a memoir?

When I was young I knew Russell's mother, Theodora, as a friend of my family and an old girlfriend of my uncle Lawrence when they went to the Haskell Indian School in Kansas. I knew her as a great dancer and full of fun. Later, when I was in graduate school at the University of South Dakota, she was a supportive friend and elder from the Yankton Sioux Tribe who cared about those of us who were trying to get an education. We used to eat at the campus cafeteria and gather at the downtown lounges to drum on our briefcases as she sang old-time powwow songs in our tribal language.

I want to correct here at this moment the notion that I think the memoir is useless or corrupt as genre, inferior to all others, and that those of us who write them are wanting attention for some inexplicable reason. As I read further about the function of the memoir as a literary kind, I find memoirs to be incantatory and self-entrancing and resonant, much like poetry, with their own fearless language taking their place as memory in the history of humanity, sometimes excessive and sometimes instructive.

When I asked an English department colleague about the definition of *memoir*, he told me with great confidence that "it can be anything you want it to be." I like that definition best. But he also reminded me that it might be useful to be humble, even a bit hesitant—that Mark Twain wrote his memoirs but did not allow them to be published for one hundred years. This advice was from a colleague who knew me well.

I think memoirs(including this one), nonetheless, are opportunistic and often don't concede a thing! Usually they tell you about the inner lives of people who either have no inner lives (so the writers fabricate them) or have inner lives that are so incredibly boring they are irrelevant to anyone except themselves. Memoirs are sometimes useful in creating a personal mythology the way some poetic works do. Such writing efforts may be considered worthy even if it is the case that one's motives are suspect.

It all depends upon how well the narrative sings. The above writers know how to make a narrative sing, with the possible exception of George W. Bush. His biography is simply the narrative of an upwardly mobile Yale cheerleader. It's a story that became a cruel joke and is useful only for making excuses that unwittingly reveal to his readers his blatant white-man privilege status. If you are prone to despondency, do not read his reminiscences.

Why, then, do we continue to write? And why the memoir?

Perhaps it is because when we write and read in public, the inevitable encounter with people who have ideas and insight as they move either toward resolution or the void tempts us to believe that, in fact, we are not alone as we had feared and that our fates might somehow be intertwined. Our encounters with the natural world, snakes and eagles, wars and chickens and ingrates of all kinds, suggest that we can be healed and inspired by the restorative stories of the creatures around us, and again, we know we are not alone.

I would love to believe that.

One of the things everybody can agree on is that memoirs do not always have to have some grand and glorious intention. They can be as silly or as seductive or as brilliant or as courageous as you want them to be. You can tell as many lies as you want, or you can tell your story with strict candor. You can be as fascinating or as profane as you want as you go about remembering the stuff that has made up your life. But what you have to keep in mind is that writing a memoir is one absurd and contrary and revolting way to share with others what it is you think deeply about in the hopes that they, too, will think deeply about those things.

For my taste, the best memoir of our century is *Personal History* (Knopf, 1997), the one written by Katharine Graham, the publisher of the *Washington Post*, just after the Pentagon Papers and Watergate time. I'm not the only one who has thought that. It won the Pulitzer Prize. She revealed her life as a woman of substance who rose to the occasion of taking over one of the most important publications of the twentieth century. A portrait of courage, surely.

For a while now, I've worked closely with a tribal writers' group called the Oak Lake Writers' Society, which has scheduled a four-day retreat every summer or fall for almost twenty years. Participants bring their manuscripts and poems. We have wonderful discussions and panels about the responsibility of writing as tribal people. We are teachers, editors, students, bureaucrats who work for the government or the tribe, parents, and relatives. We are sometimes unemployed or between jobs, but all of us have a commitment to learning how to write well, both in English and Dakota.

I have been extraordinarily aloof and arrogant in my opinion about writing about the self, telling the writers that unless you're going to be a poet, they ought to get outside of themselves. *Do not write me-me-me stuff! Move on.*

This scheduled retreat has been an effort on the part of some of us to get together every now and then to say what it is we talk about when we talk about "culture-based" writing. We've so far invited only tribal members of the seven bands of the Sioux Nation (Oglala, Minneconjou, Santee, Yankton, Sicangu, Hunkpapa, Sihasapa). We do that so we won't have to backtrack on so many of the subjects we take up. We know the story, and there is little prep time.

When a husband and wife team of memoirists were invited one memorable year, I was particularly contemptuous about writing "who am I" stories, saying, "who cares about who you are?" In one session, I even asked the presenters, who had been so kind as to accept our invitation to talk about their work in the memoir genre, "Don't you think this is overly self-indulgent?" Afterward, I thought, "Who do I think I am? How rude of me!"

I know better. And I have since felt ashamed of my behavior at that time. Before I went to school as a six-year-old, I learned to be polite and considerate, a training that I sometimes forget. The work done by these memoirists turned out to be a story cherished by people who have lost loved ones to early death, and it was particularly moving and revealing to our writers. They, of course, quickly began writing grief stories, which made me even sorrier about my assessment of the workshop.

16

IN MY EARLY YEARS it seemed important for my family to be agreeable. I know readers (and reviewers) of some of my earlier essays to whom this knowledge will come as a great surprise. But, in all sincerity, I say now that we were taught in our childhood home to be considerate.

We lived in several places. One was the one-roomed house of my grandparents a few steps from the creek. That is where we learned to be Dakotas. We talked to one another in our language, called each other Dakota kinship names and guarded our own and each other's privacy. This was a house built by the federal government for an elected official of the tribe, John Saul, a relative of my grandmother, a revered Santee/Yankton politician. It was a grand two-story place and was painted a startling white. My grandmother's house on the other hand closer to the creek, had only one room, and had never seen a paint brush.

We felt lucky to be at the Saul house even though the house had no water nor electricity. We used lanterns and kerosene lamps and an outdoor toilet. It was really no hardship because we went to bed when the sun went down and got up when the sun came up. At other times, I lived with my parents and seven other relatives (mother, father, three children, Uncle Ted and his son, and sometimes a grandmother) in a one-room tar-papered shack along the road to the agency. We had a huge stove that burned wood for heat and indoor cooking. In the summertime we cooked outdoors.

In these early days, how to be a good Dakota was a major focus. Abuse of any kind, verbal or physical, was unheard of in these families and no one ever laid a hand on me in anger. Once, when my impatient mother was fed up with the antics of my older sister and me, she grabbed a large wooden spoon and started after us. My father stopped her, saying, "Dakotas might beat their horses and their dogs, but *not* their children."

He was a man who did not always keep his anger in check. He was a middle child himself from a family of eight boys and one girl, a man whose major value was to tend to his duties toward his parents and his children. I do not remember him ever being angry with me. He drank a lot of booze when it was still illegal for Indians to buy it, so he was well acquainted with bootleggers, white men who prowled the reservation as scavengers. Neither my mother nor my grandmother would open the door for those men, but they were always available. We children were taught to avoid them.

My father always had twenty or thirty horses on the place, and he was sometimes as impatient with them as my mother was with us. A horse whisperer he was not. Learning to be a breeder of fine stallions and mares was his thing, not because he made any money at it, but just for pure pleasure. He was known as a fine rider who knew how to handle a horse with some authority. In his elder years he bred about a dozen beautiful paint horses that he gave to a nephew upon his death.

Everyone in the family except my mother and grandmother rode and trained horses. Sometimes my older sister and I rode these poor animals in the hot summer until they foamed at the mouth, eliciting the scolding of my grandfather. We were relentless and also loved to ride the calves at the corral when they were penned up and being weaned. We only did that when our father was gone away from the place, and as soon as we saw him coming down the road, we dashed back to the house, pretending our innocence. My sister's ambition was to be a barrel racer at local rodeos and powwows.

On one hot afternoon, the calves got out of control, and one of them kicked my sister in the face, giving her a black eye. We had to own up to our unsupervised activities. About that time, we learned to swear in English (because there are no swear words like that in Dakota) and to smoke cigarettes, rolling our own with a bag of Bull Durham we filched from our notoriously indulgent Uncle Ted or with tobacco stolen from our grandfather's pouch.

We were not the only ones horrified when we eventually burned down the chicken house. It was only a matter of time before we went too far. We could have started the whole woods on fire. That older sister and I, each other's only companions in a family of boy-children, often gave each other permission to behave badly.

We apparently did not take our Stephan Mission Catholic training, which was mercifully short, very seriously. We only went to that mission school in brief stretches when there was chaos at home or when our grandmother was not available as a caretaker or when my mother was ill. I learned to confess my sins there ("I've taken the Lord's name in vain, father"), and I remember so many absurd episodes from that childhood time. This was the place where the nuns boiled carrots and raisins together and fed them to the kids who were lighter-skinned than some of the others on the theory that we were anemic and unwell. They talked, too, about my grandmother and our "savage" homes without curtains and reading materials. I always knew they were wrong.

As I look back, I know that I abrogated all kinds of rarely enforced moral codes during those growing-up years, faking the deadly platitudes, the ideological roots of a religion that was not indigenous, stuff I did not know or comprehend. I think my unacceptable behavior was not intentional because I always wanted to be a good girl." "Wi cincina wa te wa . . . nuha," the community people would always say to my grandmother. And, of course, she believed them.

One awful Sunday, I remember standing stiffly at the altar in the Immaculate Conception Church to read the Gospel with Billy Feather at the opposite end of the altar standing at the ready to read the Epistle. I looked at Billy, a sweet friend of mine whom I thought of as a deadly bore, though we hardly ever spoke to each other. He was as serious as a trapped mouse. He grew up to be a catechist in a mission on some Arapaho reservation in Wyoming.

"In the beginning was the Word," I started, quiet and serious. "And the Word was . . . was . . . God . . . with . . . God. And the Word was . . ." At that moment I looked down from the altar to where my sister sat, her head bent, her black shining eyes staring at me. Her legs were crossed, and she was hunched down as though waiting for something. The fingers on her right hand were pinching the loose skin on her left and I could tell she was afraid. Of what?

As it turned out, of *me*.

I started again. "The Word was . . ." I tried to squelch my urge to laugh. That's what she was waiting for! Her eyes were suddenly wide, and she was looking at me with horror written all over her face. I started to giggle. "And the W-W-Word . . ." I took in a deep breath, but the giggles couldn't be held in. Billy looked over at me and wet his lips, leaning away from the lectern, to the far side, trying to hide himself.

Still giggling helplessly, I now had the attention of the scowling nuns in the front row. "Was-was with God and was . . . God . . ." I could no longer stifle the giggles but covered my face with my hands and just let it all out.

It was like I was enduring a bout with mental illness, and Sister Karen rose to her feet, stood there for a moment looking toward the old, feeble white-haired priest, then stood to her full height and gestured me to leave by a side entrance. She took the steps to the altar in one bound and completed the reading of the Gospel. My last glimpse of my sister was of her crouching in her seat like she had been struck by a rattlesnake. I was cornered in the vestibule by one of the big girls who shushed me and told me not to cry.

Years later I read "The Priest of the Sun" section of N. Scott Momaday's novel *House Made of Dawn*, which is introduced with its own reading of this biblical account: "Turning slightly, Cruz introduces The Right Reverend John Big Bluff Tosamah who intones, 'In principio erat Verbum' in a voice like a great dog and then says 'I have taken this as my text this evening. Amen brothers and sisters . . . *In the beginning was the word . . . in the beginning . . . the word . . .* now what do you suppose old John meant by that?'"

Cruz's poster to his flock in preparation for his oratory had read as follows:

Los Angeles
Holiness Pan-Indian, Pastor & Priest of the Sun
Saturday 8:30 p.m.,
"The Gospel According to John"
Sunday 8:30 p.m.
"The Way to Rainy Mountain"
Be kind to a white man today

By the time I read this, I was thirty-something (past the giggling phase) and upon reading that chapter, I was capable of grasping the long-forgotten sensations and perceptions of the lemming-like chant that so mystified me in my youth. I recognized the radical upheavals of the sixties, the failure of Christianity, and why that novel became required reading for every Indian of my generation who was capable of sustained thought. (It also won a Pulitzer Prize, by the way.)

This so-called "priest of the sun" characterization goes on for two pages in the novel, describing a congregation of relocated Indians in Los Angeles who in 1950 spoke very little English. It shows an Indian conman as he preached very much like the Dominican priests and nuns in my mission school in South Dakota, talking to me and Billy Feather and my sister and a hundred other "captured" Native children in 1940, and it was, as I say ironically now, "all Greek to us." Tosamah in the Momaday novel ends his diatribe by saying, "Good night and get yours."

If not Greek, then what? Revenge?

Indeed, the recognition of the kind of inescapable satire and phony, sleazy effort at propagandizing for some kind of "democratic" and "moralistic" education that rises out of Christianity for Native peoples has fueled all of my work since then, and it tells my readers what I think of the organized religion of the invaders and so-called conquerors. It is probably no accident that some of the political Indian scholars born in the 1930s, schooled by missionaries in the thirties and forties and fifties, became the liberal class and the lucid yet often distorted power elite of Indian studies in the following decades. And it is no accident that there are so many divergent responses to it all.

Momaday's time, and mine, in adulthood, was a time that was called the counterculture period in America, but only Indians of my generation can know the inspiration or liberation of Momaday's brilliant satirical storytelling. I'm not sure he thought of it as satire. Nor did his usual audience. Most of his readers talked about stream of consciousness and modernity in the sacred Native literatures of that time. Whatever your interpretation, Momaday was a huge influence on all of the writers of his time.

The truth is urban Indians in those days were the loneliest Americans. We could be born right here in the familiar places yet feel no stake in the national conversations taking place all around us at that earliest time. We were, I think, to become a part of a huge demographic shift that was going to swallow us all up as we grew to adults. We became the Indian studies professors, writers, and researchers who peopled what was called many years later the liberation front of the late sixties. And we learned, finally, to push against the Eurocentric bent of the academy.

At the time of these early growing-up episodes, though, they really weren't about massive disrespect for authority because there simply was no political authority. It wasn't even about the truth and justice and fraudulent love that was stoking the fires of Jack Kerouac and the Vietnam protesters. It wasn't about rebellion or reform so

much as it was a recognition by all of us born in the first decades of
the twentieth century of what had been done to Native peoples all
across the continent in the name of democracy and capitalism, religion and diversity. We were captives of a message of confusion and
faced compromises of all sorts.

Reading Momaday was a relief for many of us, and we began writing in order to analyze the absurdity called contemporary Indian life.
If our work since Momaday, and especially mine, has become a pro-
tracted sneer, what can you expect? We ceased to function as Elizabeth and Billy ceased to function after that moment at the Catholic
church's altar. As adults influenced from those early times, we have
learned quickly about the hold the troubled tribal government and
the wheezing ailment called the church has had on our lives.

The absurd authority of the colonial institutions that ran our lives
then and became the crucible for our feeble attempts to be ourselves
was omnipresent in those days. My family members were landowners (thanks to the outrageous Allotment Act of my grandparents'
day), so we often had to go to the agency to get permission for the
simplest events concerning land use. In order to cut down trees to
make logs for fencing, for example, my father had to get permission
from the white-man BIA agent at Fort Thompson. If the agent said no,
expressing what seemed to us a whimsical nature on any given day,
we simply went home with malice in our hearts and did no fencing.

There was, as you can imagine, a lot of protesting of these practices
even when the men in my family were elected to the tribal council
and learned in its committees to do the bidding of the overseers.
When the American Indian Movement (AIM) came along a decade
later, it had our attention. It galvanized a lot of people, and the number of American Indians enrolling in colleges grew substantially.
The American Indian Movement, though not often given the credit
it deserves in today's rise-and-fall nature of tribal life, described
our deficit lives and told us we could do better. Over the next years,
a rhetoric took hold across the country that argued for tribal iden-

tities and tribal fraternities. We learned about corrupt law and the paths toward either victimhood or emancipation. More specifically, we examined the nature of colonized law. When the AIM defenders began a dialogue concerning our discontent, people of my generation were not surprised at what the press began calling the "revolution-ary" tone. Astonished as others might have been by the violence of resentment shown in the defensive nature of the movement, many Indians had known all their lives of this spirit.

Decades later, now in the first decades of the twenty-first century, I have come to the knowledge that very little has changed concern-ing the policies, the controlling of Native rights in America, and the public dialogue since those days of my childhood, but it is not for lack of the mission statements of tribal entities who were now in charge of their own dialogues.

In spite of the valiant efforts of thoughtful people to understand why the colonizers' agenda remains so steadfast and why court cases seem so futile in the seeking of truth and justice, those years of pro-test continue to influence. The question of why the church has been so successful in its ludicrous story and devastating white supremacy policy remains a top priority for examination by all the tribes.

17

THE RISE OF THE Indian voice of the last few decades seems to have moved us all toward identifying the right problems in economic parity, education, and social cohesiveness. Yet colonization of the law and justice because of the failure to enact meaningful ethics reforms in government still keeps a watered-down accountability in play.

When I recently made a remark concerning the relentlessness of colonization on South Dakota reservations to an out-of-state lawyer at the murder-kidnapping trial of a now sixty-year-old AIM participant named John Boy Graham (*State of South Dakota v. John Graham*), the out-of-state lawyer agreed that the recalcitrance of what I was calling the white man's attitude and behavior toward Indians had not changed much in our lifetimes.

It was November 2011 when the most recent corrupt AIM trial began. An Indian from Canada, Graham was said to have shot and killed an activist Anna Mae Aquash, thinking she was an informant against AIM. The body of the victim was retrieved from the cold prairie ground, but no gun was ever found and the testimony centered upon unreliable witnesses who had to cover their own tracks.

The lawyer and I sat and watched the proceedings largely in silence. Later, when my lengthy conversation with this lawyer (from Harvard Law and Harvard Divinity School) got serious, we were no longer talking about the innocence or guilt of the man sitting in front of us, charged with a monstrous crime. We were not talking about the thinness of the prosecutor's case against him nor the mantra-like testimony of the FBI guys on the stand. We weren't talking about the facile cooperation of the major witnesses—aging, gone-to-seed AIMsters now astonishing everybody by testifying (or lying?) for the FBI and the State of South Dakota against themselves and each other. Instead of the case at hand, Harvard Law and I were talking politics, my favorite subject. This seemed to be the same conversation I often have had about the function of writers and scholars. "It's all politics," I say.

"There are reasons," the handsome lawyer with curly white hair says as I stare at him intently and wait for the witnesses to speak to the jury, "for why the white man cannot acquit an Indian in a political trial like this one. This is a political trial, not an historic one," he tells me. "And it has its roots," he believes, "in how differently the indigenous peoples and the colonizing peoples see themselves in the universe. And," he assures me, "it happens to the indigene all over the world, not just here. It's in the face of the colonizer."

"But," I ask in desperation, "will we ever know the truth about who did the kidnapping and killing of an Indian woman so many years ago?"

"No," he assures me again. "This is not about truth seeking."

I had a notion to believe him because what he was saying answered the question for me about *why* American Indian Movement trials are still being held in the Northern Plains court rooms *fully forty years after the events* occurred and at least thirty-five years after this particular crime of kidnapping and murder.

I agree that the law on Indian reservations seems to be all about control and revenge, not justice, and the length of this investigation of AIM criminals by the state and the Federal Bureau of Investigation amounts to an excessive and uncontrollable hatred and fear of Indians who are said to have committed crimes in the state of South Dakota. Indians in this part of the country are still seen as pagans in the promised land around here, unusually pathetic most times, recalcitrant and untrustworthy at the very least, and vicious criminals at most, all of whom must be punished.

Just before the Graham trial, Marty Jackley, the attorney general of South Dakota, and his people lost a case against a member of AIM who was said to be a witness to the murder of Aquash. The loss was an astonishing event, surprising the powers that be. Thus, when he took the *Graham* case to court, he admitted that he might not be able to prove who pulled the trigger.

Nonetheless, he could go to the bank with the idea that this is a state that holds a notorious vengeance against the Sioux Nation and its long-standing protests. Not to worry. The jury will do the right thing. Indeed, Graham was convicted of murder by the all-white jury with what knowledgeable people here have said was the sparsest of evidence of any trial in recent memory.

It is unfathomable to me why hundreds of thousands of dollars, millions, perhaps, have been spent by the state and federal legal systems to investigate the supposedly illegal activities committed during an affair of resistance by desperate people. Dissent? Revolution? Crime? Restorative justice? More probably, it is to publicly smear the most important and effective protest movement by American Indians in a century. AIM was probably the most significant expression of Indian rage against genocidal legislation and theft of treaty lands since Sitting Bull's days. The economic conditions on Indian reservations should tell us that this money for legal projects could better be spent on health and decent housing rather than on decades-old crimes, scenes which defy both solution and truth.

These trials that seem to go on endlessly are not so much about murder and crime and kidnapping and justice as they are about hatred and violence and revenge on the part of law-and-order systems so mismanaged and corrupt on Indian reservations that few people have faith in them anymore. Ordinary people ask: are these legitimate actions of law officers, or are they just characteristic of those who are still engage in failed colonization tactics? Are they the tactics and policies of white resentment toward the continuing presence of indigenous peoples who in historical terms were supposed to be the vanishing Americans?

The daughters of the deceased Canadian Indian woman gave countless interviews to the media, extolling their belief that the law in South Dakota convicting Graham of their mother's murder has brought "closure."

For those of us who read about injustice throughout the world, it reminded us of the decades-long efforts to pursue and silence Nelson Mandela by the white-power regime in South Africa. This was a man who spent most of his early adult life incarcerated (and, yes, probably committing monstrous crimes), simply because he would not see his country taken over by colonizers. That was a period characterized by the fear of black citizens of a white-powered nation that went on for decades. It finally ended in a modicum of peace in which majority rule, not a shared peace, thrives. There is no chance this will ever occur here because *majority rule* has an entirely different definition in Indian Country in America. As one who has taught an ugly five-hundred-year history in this country for decades, I have the dismal feeling that the end is in the beginning. That is the tragic truth.

It reminds one of the unprecedented comment made after the decades-long Watergate affair that was going on at about the same moment that the Indian movement was going on in the western states. Ultimately, Gerald Ford told us, "Our long national nightmare is over," as he pardoned the disgraced president for "any and all" crimes he may have committed. Nixon, as we all know, did not stay a day in jail for his attacks on the Constitution and went on to write several books claiming a statesman's place in the history of the United States and living a life of luxury in California and New York.

Don't tell Indians that crime, in some instances, doesn't pay.

Let's ask ourselves the question: is the "long nightmare" of the American Indian Movement trials in the state of South Dakota to be over, after forty years? The realistic answer to that question is no, and those of us interested in a just democratic future should ask *why?*

One of the reasons is that racially motivated crime and punishment here in this isolated settler place are held in the bosom of the courts, rarely in a more public setting.

There is a sizable literature on the seeking of justice and the length of the Nuremburg trials in Germany after World War II, but even that didn't take forty years to convict the Nazis in the name of justice, though Jewish prosecutors and investigators are still trying to make sense of history! That European trial, which was held rather quickly and efficiently it seemed to most of us, was a legal effort toward justice to inform the public of the rule of law. But the AIM trials seem to be of a different nature, that is, the smearing of legitimate efforts at dissent among colonized peoples. The worldwide nature of Nazi trials was a significant gesture on the part of legal scholars so that the whole world would be informed about crime and punishment in a modern setting and Germany could set out to rebuild itself. Here in the American West, Indians simply must not be given the right to their own history.

I would venture a guess that the state's fair-haired young lawyer who is now, in the first decades of the twenty-first century, prosecuting these cases (there have been four recent cases, and there are probably more to come) was hardly in elementary school when this crime occurred, studying a history without Indians, facts deliberately omitted, in his school's curriculum. No discussion of reasons for the rebellion would be advocated. This major law officer of this prairie state follows his own immigrant history of prosecuting Indians without much sense of the broader issues of colonization and racism, theft and discrimination.

The long-held hysteria of fear and hatred and violence against Indians in this region seems to be intragenerational. This is a place where the Seventh Cavalry (George Custer's old command) meets in the Black Hills every summer to recreate its world of 1870. There are television crews here in the West who put out calls for Indian "dress" and "tipis" every now and then when they want to recreate

Custer's days. Rarely does anyone get any sense that white fans of the lieutenant colonel here could possibly be racist and self-serving in dredging up as heroic a failure as that of the murderous Seventh Cavalry in the 1870s.

The Days of '76 is a bust-out celebration held annually by cowboys and rednecks and even legitimate historians at Deadwood, South Dakota. The Indian-white relationship in the West seems to be a mental aberration by people suffering from a form of hysteria or fantasy that is not unlike the urge of the excessively colonial South Africa of Mandela's time to punish people in its own land and claim superiority.

This endless protest activity and the countercharges in Sioux homelands has always been unfathomable to me. I was a young married woman when this American Indian Movement started. Now I am a grandmother. Are there ever any answers? Is it ever possible to move on? This dismal tale seems to have no end. Worse, little has changed in terms of the law and policy.

As I sat mutely in the courtroom that day in November 2011, I pondered the futility of the law in Indian Country. The killings of the AIM period are still clouded with ambiguity. It's been nearly a half century since the rise of a widespread protest movement by American Indians gave us hope for the future. Now its conclusion is a stain on the public soul and a sorrow in the Indian heart.

This trial suggested that the other side of the story could be assessed, though briefly. When the prosecutor asked the major witness against the man charged if he was fluent in the Lakota language and the witness said yes, I grimaced and whispered to my lawyer colleague sitting beside me, "Who cares? Why is that important?"

The lawyer leaned forward and said with excitement in his voice, informing me, "That's the key to your question about the relentlessness of the white man's need to go on and on and on with these charges against Indians in this case and others. It's not only about murder. It is about who you are and what you value. Your language tells you who you are, and the questioner doesn't know its rewards. He is mesmerized by what you know and what he doesn't. This trial and this narrative which will destroy one of the most important Native protests of our time is essential to his prosecutorial power and the power of the state."

The lawyer went on: "He will never stop because he can't. But, of course, he doesn't know why he does it. He deludes himself into thinking he is protecting the people."

Then, Harvard Law gave his take on why dissent by Indians who commit crimes in the defense of a cause will fail: "The question about language is a significant clue to the state's behavior, even though the prosecutor dropped it and didn't know where to go with the question or the answer. The English language, you see, is rooted in *alienation*, and so is America. Those speakers of that language are jealous and fearful of the indigenous language speakers whose language does not alienate them from the universe. It accounts for their relentlessness *to know*, and they will forever ask questions to which the answers will always be inadequate. What they can't know they must stamp out. It's based in fear," he concluded.

I fell silent as the time for our whispered conversation was coming to an end, and I was as confused as ever. And angry.

Harvard's point was that tribal people, the indigenous peoples around the world, and in this case the Lakota/Dakota/Nakota Oyate are not "unhooked" (his word) from the universe because their language "helps them to defend the intuitive knowledge of their tribal cultures against Western traditions in law, and the white man can't help but feel resentment."

I was trying to understand what he was saying: is this what some people call racism? "But," I whispered, "isn't this a political matter . . . a matter of law?"

"Yes. Of course it is. And the law which we all have to depend on, often but not always, becomes political, and so let me repeat: this is a political case. And it is bigger than John Boy. And, sadly, neither your people nor his will win it."

When he saw my face, he said, "But, hey . . . for yourself . . . I want you to read *The Cosmic Game* by Stanislav Grof. I want you to read Rumi, the mystic poet. Read Hafiz's *The Gift*. Go even further and read Parmenides. You will get it then. You will know the concepts of how a language can be rooted in *alienation* and how it can beget a racist ideology." I was remembering the many conversations I had had with people like Albert White Hat and Beatrice Medicine, Blossom Keeble, my grandmother Eliza, and so many others who also talked of the fact that the official effort to force English on us and stamp out our Dakota language brought about our own alienation.

The curly-haired lawyer said one more thing that tied it all together: "That's why your people were forced into Christianity. Because it is believed the religious experience is the way to relink with the universe. And they mistakenly believe that they can achieve the appropriate conclusions through religion. That's why a bunch of these white people right here in this room prowl the reservation homelands to attend your ceremonies. They are new to the geography, you see. So, because they do not believe they come from the land, their alienation is quite profound. The very word *religion*," he says, "*re legiaro*" (he took the pen from my hand and wrote it in my notebook), "is the Latin source for the word *religious* and what it means is 'to relink' with the universe. You Indians don't have to be the seekers that they are because it is your language which expresses your connection to the universe and to this place, specifically . . ." He waved his arms. The bailiffs began to stare at us and we fell silent. At recess time, I was called aside by the judge and told that he would not tolerate our whispering, and if we continued, we would be ejected from the courtroom.

I looked about the room and saw several local lawyers seated among the forty to forty-five spectators, recognizing one of them who had been at a Sun Dance that I attended for my cousin's piercing at Grand River years ago. There was a non-Native representative from the provincial government of Canada who had told me earlier that it was "just personal" that he was here. Nothing official. A chubby lawyer from Massachusetts watched the proceedings with great interest. He told me later that he represented for a decade some of the Indians involved in the legal matters of AIM, even Leonard Peltier, the Native man who is now serving life imprisonment for killing FBI agents. He wanted me to know that it was not true that he had been fired by the Peltier group.

The Associated Press guy could hardly wait to get out of the stuffy courtroom to his computer. Even a reporter from the South Dakota public radio was present, an indication that the media would try to be unbiased. A guy who used to do sports but is now a local TV anchor looked bored but determined. All of these writers, including myself, were busy scribbling notes.

In a surprising and stunning move, the prosecution rested without calling some of the expected witnesses. In the same moment, the defense rested without calling any witnesses at all. We, the spectators, expecting more information, were in shock.

The jury looked tired. I didn't know it then, but they were to deliberate only a few hours before they found the defendant *guilty as charged* with no murder weapon, faulty forensics, prosecution witnesses who told lies that even the spectators knew were lies, unexplained contradictions. The major Indian investigator, risen through the FBI ranks to the pinnacle of tribal government as superintendent, smiled, a pudgy little man divorced from his wife of many years and now married to the major witness against the defendant, and was congratulated in the hallway. The holes in these proceedings were like the Grand Canyon.

As I walked into the sunshine that afternoon, my out-of-state lawyer mentor had disappeared. I have not seen him since, but I have had occasion to think of him often.

18

THE ISSUE OF HOW to protest a colonial government on Indian reservations has been troubling ever since the beginning treaties were signed and colonial law emerged in full force. Indian Americans were not voters in the American political process until 1924, and tribal nations had no access to the court system until twenty years after that. As might be expected, many protests have followed this course of events.

Much of the country has come to think that the Federal Bureau of Investigation has the right, even the obligation, to be the guardian of law on treaty lands and that the U.S. Congress, from which all law emerges for the indigenous peoples of the country, can hold tribal land in trust, passing whatever legislation they deem necessary without the consent of the people. A continuous protest of these measures has been the norm. Sooner or later, though, human beings, even colonizers and indigenous people, have a tendency to come to their senses, and that means there is hope for all of us.

Historians tell us that even Woody Guthrie, now thought to be the original protester, at one time toured the country in a chauffeured car, bought and paid for by politicians, to sing the praises of the water and power barons who were devastating the western lands mostly occupied by snakes and lizards and Indians. Woody came to his senses and became a major spokesperson for ecological justice, so it is possible for the carriers of Indian law to do so too. We must not give up hope.

It is unfortunate that the narrative of the American Indian Movement has been so thoroughly debased, not only by the behavior of some of its supporters and leaders but also by its essential enemies, state governments and the federal legal establishments of the country and, of course, midwestern settlers and whites. At the beginning of the movement, Native people were gathering to protest the theft of Indian lands and the flooding of hundreds of thousands of acres protected by treaty (for hydropower), termination laws of the 1950s, poverty, devastating mining practices, and the removal and extermination policies of the modern century, to say nothing about the grim urbanization schemes and Christian boarding schools forced upon them. Protests against all of this and more gained little agency in the historical rendering of any narrative and so the beginning became the end.

This does not mean that the story of the destruction of the modern and most visible protest called AIM is now welcomed in the minds of many observers. Indeed, even many Indians call the destruction of the movement a good thing, agreeing with the major thrust of state power and interests. An acquaintance of mine from a rather conservative neighboring tribe, historically known to be fearful of the power of the Sioux (they say), emailed me as we attended the trial: "AIM became a big bust because it was started by felons who had nothing better to do than sit in there [*sic*] cells all day and dream up what would be best for the people and how they could cash in. A felon is a felon."

This, sadly, became a popular version of this historical period, but not for me.

In contradistinction, I want to think about and put forward the idea that every political and historical movement that I know of in Indian county or anywhere else has been conducive to a life of truth telling. Dissent, after all, is deeply honored as a democratic achievement, and it certainly has been a major facet of Dakota Sioux culture traditionally.

This Western tradition seems to be so if you are talking about the American Indian Movement of the 1960s or Sitting Bull's protest against the Allotment Act in the 1880s or the protest by those Indians who started the Congress of American Indians to alleviate endemic poverty in 1940 or even the teacher's association in Wisconsin that opposed Republicanism in 2017. Hundreds more come to mind. My experience tells me that it's only when internecine "civil" war prompted by colonial law and settler interest intervenes in these Indian movements that murder and assassination and savage events began to occur among the participants.

I cannot help but wonder what will happen on these homelands where we were born (the nine reserved enclaves in this state), when state law and the FBI take over completely and we are totally helpless to mobilize those who would like to protect the truth; who will dissent? Who will our children be when it is finally realized that governing a people against their wishes and needs is unsustainable, that people will not remain beggars forever? Nor will the downtrodden be silent.

It is not up to me to try to get into the minds of the accused in such trials as this one, nor am I equal to the tyrants who take law into their own hands, which, in my view, includes not only the accused AIM murderer but the lawyers and investigators who design these legal trials for their own will. In defense of all those who participated thirty years ago in the American Indian Movement in good faith, I must say they must continue to be wary. Tyrants are appearing these days as postcolonialists, and unless they are recognized and called out by those next in line, we will all be overwhelmed by their perfidy.

Over the years, I have written about these matters, trying not to be too long-winded and overwhelmed. Some say I and other writers like me have not succeeded. But most will agree that the American Indian Movement achieved a wide array of support (and still does), even though there were (and are) many Native writers and scholars, with the exception of poets, who have given up hope for substantial change. I have been grateful, therefore, for the promotion of and defense of the right of all of us to analyze and dissent, evident in the works of the most important tribal writer of our time, Vine Deloria, a brilliant attorney who rarely practiced law but always came to the rescue of free thinkers.

Once when I visited with him in Denver, he deplored the notion that many Indian lawyers say they are too busy to write for the law journals that come out of academia. It was his opinion that because of the ability to dissent that is built into the legal profession, he felt their contribution could be not only insightful but essential. He urged their participation in all forms of dialogue.

He told me that it was his experience that many judges will go to their law clerks and ask them to find out what is written by Native scholars on a given subject, and when they can't find anything, the judge often makes his decision without Indian input. This, he thought, helped to account for many wrong decisions in the law.

We agreed that in addition to the lawyer's necessity as speaker for the people, the poet is also the carrier and the repository of the people's memory even though the poet, unlike the lawyer, is usually self-appointed. The possibility of the importance of the poet makes me regret to say that I don't do much poetry anymore. Long before I ever thought about being a poet, though, I recognized that poetry like our ancestors knew is probably only rarely accessible these days. My dismal message to my students is this: go ahead and write poetry, but don't write poetry of hope. Try not to be too fanciful. Just keep the doors open.

The American Indian Movement, I would like to think, had its origins in what we in America call poetry and the law, in dissent and civil disobedience, all of which often arise out of a breakdown of organized systems in the context of totalitarian regimes. The inadequacy of the movement's ability to bring to those governed by oppressive regimes (namely American Indians), some relief from alienation is one of the tragedies of the twentieth century.

As I examine the consequences of the ubiquitous and ongoing and never-ending trials of AIM participants, Indians both on the reservation and off seem to be in a situation whereby the bureaucratic polity of government leaves little structure for dissent or civil disobedience to be asserted except through violence, convulsive shifts from paternalizing to vengeful and punitive justice. *Dissent* is not a just a word that means a refusal to conform to authority. It is the root word for *dissertate* which means to discourse at some length, sometimes formally, sometimes learnedly, sometimes haphazardly but always in order to put forth theses or ideas or theories or opinions that are in disagreement with the doctrines or usages of established thought; that's where poetry and the law and the dissertation will flourish.

No democratic society can thrive without dissent, yet America expects Indian nations, almost always on the verge of collapse before and since 1934, when severely limited tribal governments were initiated as a means of destruction and colonization, to do so. The effort of Native people to fight for the freedoms that other people take for granted—the right to defend nationhood and histories, languages, land, treaties and the human spirit—must be recognized as the right of all human beings. This is the human right that is deemed so precious to civilized societies.

I was still engaged in a failing marriage and living in New Mexico when, in 1961, Indians met at a Chicago conference to produce a Declaration of Indian Purpose, a dissent of its own kind. This conference was an inadequate cry for help often led by those with nothing to lose, people who were very probably ill-equipped to take on the responsibility for such an undertaking, but we all knew, even those of us who were taking our little children to the libraries and the inadequate schools, taking care of aging parents in inadequate housing, getting in our cars and driving away from the miseries in front of us and struggling with our own personal cries for help, that it had to happen. The inevitability of it did not strike me until many years later.

Thus, it took a long time for individuals as well as the movement itself to coalesce, and by the time it did, too much celebrity had invaded the leadership, bringing with it the inevitable corruption and selfishness. Even as we watched our TV sets showing us the first steps of American astronauts on the moon, however, we knew that the emergence of the kind of organized indigenous dissent at the Chicago conference meant to all of us that the strains that had existed for a hundred years in Indian Country were no longer tolerable.

Strains of alienation were now out in the open: anti-Indian legislation; ongoing land thefts; manipulation of resources by governments and commercial concerns; poverty; destruction of environments; theft of water rights; a flooding of villages and cemeteries against the wishes of the people; oppressive school systems run by priests, nuns, and military personnel; violence; discrimination; and exclusion from democratic participation in the works of the surrounding world all challenged what we wanted our futures as Indians in America to be.

The decades preceding the emergence of the dissent exemplified by such meetings as well as the forthcoming American Indian Movement. Historically, the decades of 1940 and 1950 were among the most restrictive years for American Indian populations who were, in spite of it all, no longer "vanishing" but fast becoming the "surviving" peoples in American society. Men and women were in the military and then came home to joblessness. Endemic poverty, infant death, raging diabetes, obesity, and tuberculosis and a stunning death rate in all categories were indications of a slow death to a people who had tried to live successfully in the Northern Plains for centuries but who could now no longer survive.

Political movements like AIM were not only dramatic challenges to the existing social order so carefully managed by mainstream America but were inevitable just as other social upheavals were taking place across the globe. I am not aware of how many of the youthful readers of this book are familiar with the 1985 issues of apartheid and genocide in colonial South Africa, but many of the concerns and chaotic upheavals in that country, also a long time in coalescing, fit with the concerns involving indigenous populations in America. The struggle with colonial law and order brought profound violence to many peoples, including American Indians and Africans, during those years.

When I read somewhere that white South Africans were saying well into the 1980s, "We fear blacks in our country because if they are free of colonial rule, we will be punished for all the wrongs we have committed," I recognized the fear of white Americans and especially those in South Dakota who were being confronted with the Supreme Court decision concerning the Black Hills land issue, that it was a "theft," not a "taking" in legal terminology. The 1980 Supreme Court writings put the notion of misplaced legal authority starting as early as 1877 on the table after decades in the courts. The resentment and backlash by whites was vicious throughout all tribal enclaves.

The same sentiment—"we will be punished"—has been expressed by the white farmers and ranchers and European capitalists who took over the American West without the consent of indigenous landowners who had lived there for centuries. The phrase "if they are free of our colonial rule" posed many ugly possibilities for the colonizer, though there was little real discourse between the groups.

Thieves, it was speculated, might have to pay, turn over huge tracts of land to their original owners, so that tribes could at long last develop appropriate economic systems. In the case of the Sioux, the dialogue revealed, America could not steal 7.7 million acres of their property and then wonder why their victims are poor. Legal scholars and early settlers, it was speculated, might have to give up their glorified positions in history to be condemned as corrupt, violent promoters of apartheid and genocide, thieves and murderers. New sovereign First Nations governments on Indian lands might have to be designed to replace the colonial ones. This revelation of the possible disgrace of America's fantastical past was almost too much to bear for the settlers and citizens of the vast western territories, and the reaction of powerful white interests was quickly amassed.

They turned to the courts for recourse, and many unsatisfactory laws were in the making.

In some areas, though, the tide was turning. South Africa elected its black revolutionary hero Mandela, who had committed many crimes during his revolutionary period, to the presidency. He was still called a monster by the white regime's power base, but his power was in the people. A solution was found in Thabo Mbeki, a former terrorist and dissenter and revolutionary black leader who had stood beside his country's hero to lead violent dissent for decades and who surprisingly became the leader of this country. This was a leadership that rose out of tribalness and violence and was almost unheard of and unaccountable in its transformation, a miracle of the modern world.

More than any country in all of the continent, South Africa has continued to try to shed its colonial instincts and join the democrats of the globe who desire to live peaceably and in harmony with other nations. It proves that the failure of colonization does not mean catastrophe. It proves that historical crimes don't always pay. And it proves that enormous changes can occur.

To propound that theory is not my purpose here because, in spite of all that we know, Mandela-like leadership in Indian America seems to be the missing ingredient. Perhaps the lack of a grand movement toward freedom based in such astounding leadership is the intrinsic characteristic and quality of tribal societies like ours, which cannot move away from the nature myths and trickster tales that account for our origins rather than seeking widespread consensus and power.

That disadvantage may be what distinguishes the American Indian from the African example as well those nations that emerged from the Roman empire of ancient times into contemporary nations. In the Northern Plains small, fragmented survivors of a holocaust are overwhelmed, as some three hundred First Nations exist now when thousands had existed at the time of the arrival of Europeans and a whole new global perspective was coming into sight. War and national conquest in the human communities of the world has always existed, and change is always a struggle. There is nothing new about war and theft, only the remedies. Perhaps looking to the indigenous past is a way to find solutions. As I am always saying, history matters.

There is a Dakota story that tells of how the Rees, long-time neighbors of the Sioux, had been the owners of Sacred Corn since time immemorial and of how they worked with their neighbors to come to agreements concerning their futures. They were a small tribe, relatives of the Pawnees, living on the fringes of the great lands of the powerful Sioux Nation. Corn was as sacred to the Rees as the pipe was to the Sioux.

Keyapi. Once, they say, when the Sioux had taken Corn from the Ree homelands, not knowing it was theirs (they say), war was possible. There was a Sioux man named Matohoshina who went to the Rees with tobacco and told the Rees about their sorrow and shame and that they wanted to have a lasting friendship with the Rees. They admitted they had done this bad thing about which they were remorseful.

The Sioux told the Rees about their own remedy, a ceremony called Hunkapi, the "making of relatives," which could avoid a terrible war in which the Rees were sure to be killed in great numbers. They performed the ritual for their neighbors using the tobacco in the sacred way and from that time on, a lasting friendship was bonded: the Rees shared the Sacred Corn and the Sioux shared the sacred pipe and the essential buffalo, symbol at the heart of nationhood.

I have found that it is not always so easy to come to terms as is suggested in this story. Little survives from those times, *except the story*, and that is what is important in the retelling of it!

It is true that as citizens of a modern great Sioux Nation we have lost much, and as individual Native persons we have lost too. Nonetheless, I wake up every morning to the sun and tell myself how lucky we all have been as survivors of the ugly colonial history remembered in these pages! Everything changes, and adjustments are hard, yet it is important for me to acknowledge that any of the sweeping changes that have happened since I graduated from college and entered into an academic life are for the better.

I have just started to lose my faith in proverbs and ceremonies. Today, people who know me well think of me as an unbeliever. A cynic. I don't know how to account for this way of being yet, in spite of the ironic title of this memoir. I don't think often of the collateral damage one suffers for being a Dakota in America. It is just a reality. "Being an Indian," the old folks I grew up with said, "is hard."

Life is an interesting journey of soaring and sweeping and darting and floating. My life is a good one probably more the result of my good luck than my persistent nature. I often say that the academic life is a fruitful one, and I have had to admit it is my personal life decisions rather than my professional ones that have probably been fraught with disappointment.

19

I CANNOT SPEAK OF good luck without acknowledging that I have occasionally been in the right place at the right time.

When the national movement called Affirmative Action in Academia was put in place as a national imperative to include American Indians in the academies of learning and professionalism in which they had only been clients and subjects, I had already returned to South Dakota. The developers of the national effort initiated the recruitment of enrolled members of tribal nations with teaching credentials for an opportunity to enhance their credentials and join the academy. I was recruited and saw it as a good luck event.

While it was the perfect solution to my failing marriage, it also coincided with my acknowledgment that this federal government's interest in bringing American Indians into an educational environment from which they had been exempted for two hundred years was a civil rights initiative. Civil rights movements were fostering change across the land and it was a time of much learning. With my interest as an adult observer in contemporary political matters and as a member of a rather active tribal political family, I was not unconnected to the civil rights movements and the perspectives of social change that seemed unstoppable in the ideological moments of the sixties and seventies and eighties.

My sense of anxiety and foreboding was not just that my marriage was coming undone; it was also that I had been teaching in a high-risk part of the Southwest. Integration in the schools in southern

New Mexico was in a state of chaos and revolution. Well-meaning people were saying things like, "When we integrated our schools . . ."

What? What? I would look at them in amazement.

Integration was *not* what was taking place in these southern and western cities and rural areas at that time.

The denial of that reality was everywhere. Grade schools and middle schools in all of New Mexico were still segregated, as was every high school except one in the downtown area where I lived. Spanish-speaking students were segregated in schools where they lived, African American students and Indians went to schools in their segregated neighborhoods, and there was much denial of what was really taking place in educational circles. Housing was a major obstacle.

The federal law called termination and relocation had forced an unready, unskilled, hostile urban Indian population onto the scene. It was an urbanization plan by the federal government to remove Indians from their rather substantial homelands and groom them to be part of the American mainstream. It was touted as a grand opportunity for poor people.

Nothing in the curriculum seemed relevant as we asked students to read Keats poetry and the stories of Herman Melville. Class content was severely censored in the English department where I taught high school classes, not only because of political unrest, but because people were resistant to the changes in social and political matters and even religious matters as well. As an example of this censored version of American life and experience, we were teaching Shakespeare in our sophomore classes to students who hardly spoke even American English let alone the rather stilted dramatic English of the 1600s. Still, we were expected to avoid the *Romeo and Juliet* play because of its "sexual" themes. We could assign other plays (*A Midsummer Night's Dream*, for example), but not the teenaged romance of Romeo and Juliet which might have, at the very least, caught students up in a fantasy of their own age-group. The social classes of religionists so prevalent in the southern part of the country looked with fear toward what was being taught and learned in a dramatically changing society.

One teacher of my acquaintance tried to teach *Romeo and Juliet* without sex in much the same way we often taught *Othello* without race. She gave it up and went back to Hawthorne and Hemingway. When the movie *Romeo and Juliet* was released, born-again Christians just removed from the failing coal miles of Arkansas to the sunny Southwest met with faculty members to show their great concern, protesting the assigned readings with the feared change in sexual mores in mind. The faculty had wanted to take students to a downtown theater for an afternoon showing, but the hullabaloo that idea caused in the community was so vicious they found themselves surrounded. Meetings were called, students were absent from classes, pickets showed up outside the school grounds.

There was even a backlash when I assigned the works of black, chicano/a, and Native writers in my classes and asked students to write reaction papers. One white student handed in a blank sheet with this comment, "I don't give a damn to read this stuff." At the time I had little notion of how to handle such a reaction, so I just put a big black F on the paper and handed it back.

Unaccountably, other events were indicative of my isolation from such communities, and I sought out my own social and intellectual life. I was going to the library and checking out books on the Plantagenet kings of England for no reason at all except escapism and intellectual curiosity. I made great lists in my notes of the genealogies and wars and movements of the era of aristocracy in England as though any of this mattered. There was literally no place to turn. This is called avoidance behavior in the social sciences. Many of us were just trying to avoid what was really happening in this turbulent time.

Nobody was talking about postmodernism or "third-world-ism" yet, at least not in the educational circles in New Mexico. My husband, from Cheyenne River Reservation in South Dakota, was working at a local newspaper, refusing to talk about the real thing. He started taking our children hiking in a strange place called Sitting Bull Park every Sunday, but we never did get an answer to our queries about its name. I had students with heavy southern accents whose parents had been moved from the failing coal mines of West Virginia to the potash mines of New Mexico, and all they wanted to read was Mark Twain. Our first school play in October was to be a classic. It was the first and only time I ever heard the play *Julius Caesar* acted with southern West Virginia accents, and I thought I would roll in the aisles with laughter.

I had to face the truth. I was a stranger in a strange land.

Things at home were becoming more bizarre, violence now out in the open. Finally, in the spring, I put my husband's things in paper boxes and set them outside of the locked door of our home. Like a Lakota man with some vague sense of class or tradition, he came and got his stuff and we never spoke to each other again. Divorce in traditional Native societies can take on its own grief, so in recognition of the past, I never consulted a lawyer.

Driving north in a U-Haul with four children, a dog and a cat, and all of my worldly goods, a twenty-dollar bill and my father's Phillips 66 gas card in my pocket, it seemed like a way out. My father met me at Lusk, Wyoming, and for the first time I noticed his missing teeth, his long unkempt graying hair straggling over a threadbare shirt, and the dull fear in his eyes as he looked at this remnant of a family now homeless and demoralized. We found a three-bedroom rental in the hills, he bought a washer and dryer for me and his grandchildren, and he gave me money for the first and last month's rent.

At the time, my father was ranching on the Crow Creek Indian Reservation in South Dakota as he had always done and had sold cattle to help my mother buy a house in a nearby town. This meant that my mother was not living with him on a permanent basis on the reservation but kept in touch by driving to his place every other week or so with groceries. My now estranged husband, his own integration coming on slowly, paid no child support and did not try to contact us. His silence was a relief. My mother had no words of advice for me, but my father's words of admonishment were that a man who does not take care of his children cannot be called a man.

At the end of their lives, my mother moved back to my father's place to take care of him when he got very old and sick. This indicated for me, as a child of abrupt and confusing change, a class act on the part of my mother because her marriage to this man who was not considered good husband material was a struggle. An adulterous man who had often betrayed her, he was selfish and often had disappeared from our home life for days at a time. She had been on her own for much of their time together. Her style was true blue, though, in lots of unnoticed ways. He was a man who displayed his own kind of decency, a loner, a drinker, a man who took great care with his parents and his children, his cattle, and horses in terms of basic necessities.

They were both thrilled when I got a job teaching English in the largest high school in South Dakota, where drug use was out of control and where I was trying to ignore it all by setting about rearranging my life. I put my children in school and cried every night, not because I wasn't happy to leave a dreadful marriage, but because I felt sorrow for a dream gone bad. I remember unpacking a clay table model of a very old Asian man and woman seated at a seaside pier, he setting out the fish just caught and she holding up a garment for repair. My husband and I had bought it when we were together and still had the dream. Tears filled my eyes. The children and I bought school clothes with borrowed money and the dog chewed up a pair of new school shoes even before school started. I cried again.

What can save us from the fatalism of a marriage gone bad? Women have asked themselves that question for ages. The truth is marriage helped me grow up, and I don't know of any other action that could have done so. I was a very spoiled child in the sense that I was always the youngest girl-child in a family of many boy-children, and until that time I had accepted few real responsibilities. There was always someone there to pick up the pieces for me, particularly an older sister who now lived thousands of miles away.

I was on my own now and frightened.

I walked for an hour every morning just before dawn, noticing that the scented air from the pine trees of the sacred Black Hills was welcoming me home. The pale moon trying to take its night leave settled on the horizon at the end of the day, and the Canadian geese were flying each morning, and those realities gave me some comfort. It was autumn and the leaves were falling, and I often felt profound grief for my children who would not know their father and for their father who would not know his children. I had left him, and no one, not even his sisters or brothers, knew where he was for decades.

One could get maudlin thinking these thoughts about divorce and its aftermath, so, being a person who more or less takes life as it comes, I dredged up an old cowboy song my uncle used to sing when he was drunk after his wife had left him. I sang it out loud — "Thank God for Greyhound, she's gone!" — hoping the people sleeping in the houses nearby wouldn't hear me. To make myself feel less disappointed as a participant in this colossal failure, I made myself believe that my soon-to-be ex-husband was singing it too. Today, I still hope he was, but we had no contact with him. His death twenty years later left us with no way to know for sure.

At his death he was brought back by his sister to Timber Lake for burial. I'm told they gave him a military burial. His children now possess his silver star and his two bronze stars from World War II and Korea.

I truly have never looked back with any kind of insight.

We stayed one year in a rented house and then moved again. This time I put my threadbare belongings in my mother's basement (where they remained for the better part of a decade), and I went off with four kids in tow, the aging dog, and the now overweight cat to a graduate program at the University of South Dakota — an affirmative action program for Natives who were enrolled members of federally known tribes and holders of undergraduate degrees. There were very few of us in those days, so I was sought out by people who were taking the notion of affirmative action seriously.

I had not intended to do this, but when Jim Emery, an old friend of my parents and a community leader, and another friend, Harry Eagle Bull, a BIA official from the Aberdeen Area Office, dropped in on me after one of my English classes in Rapid City to tell me about the chance to apply for a master's program at the University of South Dakota, I couldn't ignore this once in a lifetime chance. This program, a function of a national effort, was designed to bring Indians into the school systems as counselors to stem the dropout tide in high schools.

I never did become a counselor, but I took the degree. In this program I met such people as Lionel Bordeaux, who eventually became the charismatic and steadfast president of Sinte Gleska University on the Sicangu Indian Reservation in South Dakota. He has been an internationally recognized leader in Indian education. More than anyone I know, he has proven Thomas Wolfe's admission that "you can't go home again" to be false. The truth is we all go home again.

My kids and I drove into the little college town, Vermillion, with high hopes. This place was then and still is an ugly little university town in the middle of what used to be (before white settlement) some of the most interesting prairie landscape and fluvial river landscape in the West. It still tries to be that. Skunks are roaming in people's backyards. Threatening cyclone storms cloud the sky every afternoon. The smell of hog farms and silage feeding areas for cattle sometimes takes over.

One of the first people I met there was Eugene Sekaquaptewa from Hopi. I can't imagine what he thought of the place, coming in from the desert country. His daughters were the ages of mine, and we all quickly settled into an academic world that had some Indians other than ourselves in it.

My idea at the University of South Dakota at that time was that I would do graduate work to get a better paying teaching job that would allow me to take care of my family. I had no idea how isolating that experience in graduate studies at the University of South Dakota would be for me. I am hesitant to say this is where I learned to mix a really good orange juice and vodka screwdriver and started smoking cigarettes again.

There is very little architecture at that prairie college town to remind you of who you are as an Indian, but there was a collective of twenty or so tribal people struggling on a journey toward knowledge, and I am grateful for the educational opportunity. This is where I met CJ Lynn, from the Spokane Indian Tribe in Washington State, who was to become my soul mate. The first time I saw him I thought he looked like one of the Traversie brothers from Eagle Butte, my ex-husband's relatives, and I tried to avoid him.

CJ, also a seeker of a master's degree, wrote many grants for his tribe, ran successful programs for them later on the reservation, and did his service as a tribal judge for several years. Much later he assisted the tribe in rewriting its tribal constitution.

This program, the result of affirmative policy initiatives, has been considered highly successful since all of the participants have fed into the educational and political systems and have made a huge difference in the notion that Native peoples must be in charge of their own intellectual destiny. Many writers and educational and business leaders have emerged from those years of opportunity. At the same time, Dr. James Wilson, a Sicangu educator with degrees from Arizona State University, accepted a DC job in the Office of Equal Opportunity in the Kennedy administration and was responsible for getting dozens of American Indians into the legal professions of the United States. Such efforts have changed the Indian world.

20

IT WAS NOT LONG before I began writing in defense of indigenous affairs, especially after I completed my graduate studies and became a college professor. "Publish or perish" has great meaning in the field of university teaching, and I would never have lasted for twenty years at Eastern Washington University without my dedication to writing and publishing.

Not all went as well as planned, though. The Indian studies enclave at the university had a series of false starts and several directors. One professor-director, coming out of California and claiming to be Aleut, proved an out-and-out fraud, which was almost unheard of then but is now known to be—if not common in university life—at least quite occasionally uncovered and written about by some of us.

The Indian studies component at Eastern had started with the gathering of several Northwest Indian professionals who made up the Native board of regents, giving advice and developing historical perspectives in curriculum never before developed at a state university. People from the powerful indigenous tribes of the area such as Spokane, Colville, Nez Perce, Yakima, Umatilla, Flathead, and Kalispel were engaged.

Leroy Seth of the Nez Perce Tribe of Idaho, an alumnus of EWU and a well-known basketball player, was the chairperson of this successful group for several years. We knew him also as a handsome and accomplished champion fancy dancer famous at the war dances and wacipis throughout the Northwest. When I retired, he was still dancing, cool as ever, and those of us who knew of him called him the oldest Indian fancy dancer in the known Indian world.

At EWU we had initiated a vital curricula sketched out with such scholars as Mary Nelson (Colville), Dr. James Somday (Colville), Dr. Cecil Jose (Papago and Nez Perce), and several others when it finally occurred to us in our committee meetings that our director, the Aleut from California, was not up to the challenge.

First of all, he could not write a decent paragraph for the many course outlines and documents to get our courses through the faculty senate committees. How, we asked ourselves and each other, could he be a professor in our field with such poor academic skills who never taught any of our classes? We had talked among ourselves for some time about whether or not we should investigate but were hesitant to take action.

The Indian faculty and board had nothing to do with his hiring, a protocol in the discipline that has changed considerably since those early days, so we had taken it on the administration's word that he had appropriate credentials. The administration had, apparently, taken the word of unnamed others who seemed reliable to them. This meant that there had really been almost no vetting in his hiring process.

One afternoon, after one of our frustrating faculty meetings when we were presented with his paperwork on class description and rationale that was assigned to me for rewriting, I was fed up. I was more than a little angry at the director's incompetence, which he often covered up with his arrogance and good looks.

I left the meeting early, went to my office, and dialed up the office of the registrar at the University of California, San Diego, to check up on this director's claim to have scholarly credentials from that institution. Nobody with a master's degree in psychology, which was his claim, could be this incompetent, I thought. At the very least, one should be expected to write a coherent paragraph.

The waiting at the phone seemed endless, and I was about to hang up when a voice on the other end said, "Sorry, Professor Cook-Lynn, this person matriculated here some years ago and left after two semesters. *No degrees were earned."*

I was stunned.

I sat in my office gazing out of the huge plate glass window as the sun cleared the roof of the administration building and went westward. Without thinking it through, I went straight to my dean's office with this calamitous news. He listened. He said he would immediately contact the provost.

Still not thinking very clearly, I walked to the Inuit from California's office. "Can I come in and close the door?"

"Sure."

"Sir, is there some reason that when I called the officials at San Diego, they tell me you have no degrees and that you left there before your freshman year was completed?"

"What?" He swung his chair around so his knees were almost touching mine. "What?"

He seemed genuinely shocked.

He looked into my eyes and said, "Liz, there must be some mistake. There must be! Listen, I will call them and get this straightened out."

He patted me on the shoulder as he walked me to the door.

"Don't worry," he said, as if consoling me.

Leaving his office with my knees shaking, I walked back to my office and sat down. When the phone rang I didn't answer it.

Holy max, I thought. *What have I done? Accusing the director of the one kind of fraud that is actually an academic crime? Good grief! I've even gone to the dean.*

I quickly walked to my car and drove away from the campus. I hardly spoke as my children and I prepared dinner.

The next morning I drove into my parking space with great dread. I went to my class, the Short Story, English 220, and talked about Anton Chekhov. Did you know he was more than a dramatist? He actually published hundreds of short stories.

A colleague in the English department called me for lunch.

I still had heard nothing.

After lunch as I was walking back to my office, I met the provost on his way to the dean's office. He was an incredibly ambitious tweedy man who stopped me and with his face inches from mine, his finger poking me in the chest several times, said, "We have had several meetings. If any of this gets out to the *Spokesman-Review* newspaper, your program in Indian studies is gone!" His eyes were red and he was trying to hold in his fury.

"But, sir, how is it he has been here five years and received many grand citations?"

"Let me tell you again, Liz, there is to be *no* publicity about this! None! Nada! Do you get it?"

He left me standing there.

The director of Indian studies was gone within a week, a laudatory recommendation from the university in hand, quickly landing a job in DC to assist in the planning for the new Indian museum on the mall. He was said to be earning a six-figure salary. There was an early interview in the *Washington Post* as he was welcomed into the academic community of the nation's capital in Indian affairs. I knew some people who knew Dick West, the Cheyenne Indian director of the museum, and I thought about calling them. But I did nothing, the provost's warning ringing in my ears.

I heard later from one of my students at EWU that she had known the now disappeared director when she was a student at Chemawa Indian School in Oregon, where he was a counselor, and that he had absconded with some student funds they had raised from bake sales. She was giggling that he had finally been found out and went away to spread the news.

Was there no end to the pettiness of this man? Stealing bake sale money? From students? Was there no end to the chaotic nature of our work as Indian professionals who had struggled so hard to see this program come to life? I was angry but felt powerless. When I talked to the dean about why the university had sent this man on to greater vistas with a laudatory recommendation based in fraud, he said the man had threatened a law suit, and the administration wanted to avoid further controversy. I said nothing more.

This was the first real opportunity I'd had, in all my years of academic work, to begin to understand all the underground men and women we know and meet in academia who decry the social chaos for which we are all just as responsible as anyone else but do nothing about it. This was the first time I truly understood that character in Fyodor Dostoyevsky's *Notes from the Underground*, a man who was a useless academic, a learned person who accommodated corrupt power structures in Russia in the name of some kind of ideals or needs or "common good," a man who becomes a limited person. "Neither hero nor insect," the character describes himself. I had become one of them.

When someone from the *Washington Post* called me up months later to ask about some "rumors" that had apparently followed the director, I told her everything I knew, thankful to be able at last to tell someone, anyone! I gave her permission to use my name; I even gave her other names to contact, but nothing ever came of it. The tragedy is that we are the people who stay silent and doom not just ourselves but our tribal nations.

In the academic world, a society deeply divided by class and politics and status and ambition, there is no shame in trying to escape its shortcomings. There is no price to pay and no humiliation in the eyes of professionals as long as methods of silence can prevail. It was not that we in Indian studies wanted to be silenced, but we knew that even had we gone to the outside press concerning this outrage, we and our students and our program would still have been the victims.

Yet there is still no excuse for my cowardice.

What should I have done? I should have exposed the whole rotten mess, of course, consequences be damned. I think it is Camus who says that we should not only refuse to cooperate with fraud and corruption, we should perpetually revolt and sustain a permanent alienation from power. That's okay for the existentialists of postwar France, but what woman with four children to support is going to do that?

"There is beauty and there are the humiliated," Camus says. I felt like the latter. But the truth is no one knows shame anymore. Sometimes that includes me.

My days in an otherwise wonderfully satisfying professorship were probably numbered from that moment on. I felt weak and alienated and betrayed. I am proud that I lasted twenty years and more as a Native academic because I still think the academic life is a good one. This is where we can reproduce ourselves and our work. The question is, what mechanisms can be put in place that will show how the exploitations that began a very long time ago continue even into modern times? I know no answer to this. Perhaps it is left up to the coming generations to find answers to that question.

Nothing wipes outrages like this one from one's memory. But I excuse myself and my inability to act aggressively by thinking that you have to be a tougher, more skillful politician than I am and you have to be assisted by a team of like-minded professionals to prevail in the face of such academic weakness and subterfuge. I'm a mere teacher, and I have a subject matter to which I must be responsible, to say nothing of students who want desperately to believe in your words and the process.

Yet as I have moved on, I recognize that it is an uphill struggle on many fronts to prevail in the academy. My writing has been more aggressive than my personal acts. People have given it all sorts of descriptions, mostly that it is militant and unscholarly and unworthy of a university press. I've paid that price too.

I come from a tribe that has borne many injustices, which means that much of the time I've learned to just go with the flow. There is a huge history in my past and in the past generations, though, and once in a while the outrage really gets to me. Stifling reform and muzzling dissent will always be the way of power enclaves. The best

I can do is choose where and how I want to live. Often, in my old age, I recognize that I have the luxury now of just refusing to cooperate.

Trying to continue my work in the discipline of Indian studies, trying to publish my writings, and trying to fight the mechanisms of the dominant culture that keep Indians in poverty has become the focal point of my professional work.

21

IN 2010, YEARS AFTER this event concerning the corrupt director at EWU, I read a story in the *New York Times* of how the "Execution of Dakota Indian Nearly 150 Years Ago Spurs Calls for Pardon" and thought about how even the very innocent are exploited. This is a story that was finally hitting the airwaves after years of silence and avoidance and denial. I knew this story and asked myself, *Pardon? For what crime?*

I knew, then, why I was to become a writer. Writing, it seems, is the talent that allows us to analyze things and come to some kind of consensus about them, even if we are ashamed to squander chances and put ourselves as representatives of Indians in severe jeopardy. A horrible passivity seems visible on all fronts for some of us; yet, without writing it down, there is no analysis possible. So as I refuse to accept the stories that are told by those who have something to lose, I write.

This particular story in the *Times* tells of a Dakota man whose name was We chank wasta do(n)pe, known as Chaske, who was hanged " by mistake" by the U.S. government in the largest mass hanging in this country at New Ulm, Minnesota, in 1862. It is a story long held in the hearts of the Oyate.

The photo in the newspapers shows that in the years around 1862, thirty-eight Dakotapi (Isianti) were executed on the day after Christmas as a result of the Little Crow War. White Minnesotans had gathered for the event. They say there were ten thousand white settlers there to witness and cheer.

The trouble was, Chaske had received a commuted sentence from President Abraham Lincoln some days or weeks before the mass execution. But he was hanged anyway. "By mistake," history says. Nowadays, years after the event, it is odd that the triumphalism for justice that is typically American prevails in the public mind and only now brings up talk of a federal "pardon" for the unfortunate Indian who was innocent but hanged "by mistake."

In law a "pardon" means to pass over an offense. What offense?

That article, written by one who does not reside intellectually in a Native history, forces us to ask, how do you "pardon" a man who has done no wrong? Is it the Jesus thing? This seems to be an example of how the outside world intervenes in such histories in order to excuse history and "mistakes" ("Oh, pardon you") and touch bleeding American hearts.

Does this kind of writing and journalism pass any kind of smell test?

The article, in the usual colonial fashion of the mainstream press, claims that a pardon for an innocent Dakota man hanged mistakenly by the U.S government in 1862 is enough to cleanse the white man's behavior during a very bad historical time yet does not utter a word about returning hundreds of thousands of acres of land stolen from the Dakota Nation through malfeasance and greed at the time of the execution.

The theft of the Dakota homeland is the *real* crime here. Who is pardoned for that, and how?

Anyone who is capable of sustained rational thought knows that this story is the result of an attempt at cleansing history rather than an attempt to tell a legitimate history about what really happened. It is the kind of story that makes Mr. and Mrs. America feel better, but it does nothing to say how the Dakotas can reclaim their stolen lands and move into an economic future that does not thrive by establishing glitzy casinos to attract tourists on the fragments of land called "trust" that are still, by some miracle, in Native hands.

I will review it again here: This tribe in 2018 possesses seven thousand acres, hardly enough for a ranch spread in this part of the western country. In 1862 it possessed over three hundred thousand by treaty. These Dakota people were ranchers and farmers and had established themselves in the prairie landscape for a thousand years. Now confined mostly to homesites and casino plazas, recognize that their once-satisfying life along the rivers of middle America has undergone dramatic change.

Why not tell the story of how their land was taken from them? What about land reform and the reclamation of natural resources with the goal of economic security that does not depend on gambling exploitations?

The way this story is cleansed in a widely read newspaper doesn't help writers and historians who want to reconstruct real history and find solutions to social breakdown, poverty, racism, and chaos. Its main source is the Minnesota Historical Archives, a repository that is notorious among the Dakotas for being among the most biased of any repositories available to their scholars. Most thoughtful and analytical Indian writers would never in all conscience write an article like that appearing in the *Times*, which means that the feeling is probably mutual, as the *New York Times* would not be interested in hearing from them either.

The story's dateline was Mankato, Minnesota, and its reporter was Robert K. Elder, who was rewarded with a byline. As a person who studied journalism as an undergraduate, I know it's a great thing to be bylined in the best newspaper of our time. Congrats, Mr. Elder! The story was picked up by other news organizations and without appropriate Indian analysis appeared in the *Star Tribune* in Minneapolis, to be lauded by uncritical readers, both Indian and white. It filtered into the regional press enclaves. When Al Franken sat on the Indian Affairs Committee in Washington DC he said he would use his influence to promote the "pardon."

One wonders how much this senator knows of the real Indian history of his state.

Hundreds of Dakotas were held in camps near Fort Snelling, the Guantanamo-like concentration camp of the 1800s. Many of them died there, others were held for decades, and others never went home again. An innocent was hanged "by mistake."

This seems to some to be an example of the state of political and public affairs concerning the indigenous peoples of America who have been from the beginning a people headed toward either extinction or colonization. Dakotas will further disintegrate if land is not returned for the purpose of future economic development. Pardons? How inadequate!

It is not as though the Dakotas committed unforgiveable and heinous crimes and must be redeemed. These historical figures did nothing except arise from the land of their ancestors and refuse to give it up to intruders.

Americans are stuck with this kind of story as a failure of narrative, a colonization of history that permeates American life. Why are we still writing about Indians who are said to be asking for pardons when all they did was defend themselves from selfish thieves?

Instead, Indians should be asking for stolen lands to be returned and for the state governments that hate the presence of the indigenous peoples to go the way of other menacing enterprises like the Ku Klux Klan and the Citizens of the South, who hated blacks. A new history must be written and a new world with indigeneity (not colonization) leading a major moral, legal, and economic strategy. Indians who become academics and writers in a colonized world where multiethnic coalitions are set one upon another seem to be lost in history. Public policy, now in the market for "pardons," should never mean an acceptance of a colonized life.

Politicians from over three hundred surviving First Nations organized in my lifetime what has been called The Congress of American

Indians in Washington DC. It is in danger of becoming a treatise on how to fit a square peg in a round hole, if it does not stop its effort to excuse a really terrible federal policy and a false history toward Indians. This group has to understand what its function is when well-known contradictions between the colonized and the colonizer are everywhere in law and policy and little is done to set things straight.

It's not that writers from the Indian world or even politicians or even lobbyists are imprisoned these days for holding unpopular scholarly views. Indians are not forcibly exiled from the United States as are other colonized nationalists around the world, from Africa and China and Venezuela.

American Indians are simply ignored.

It's not that Indians are considered "third-world-ists," living here in America in exile with no way to go home. Indeed, many colonial politicians today believe Indians to be lucky to be assimilated survivors and participants in democracy, if they think about them as indigenous peoples at all.

It's just that to substitute a story that functions for the defense of and management of our despotic governments instead of a failed narrative asking for "pardons" for a man wrongfully put to death 150 years ago cannot impact any crisis that confronts us. The failure of state jurisdiction to protect our first-nation citizenship and the treaty relationship to federal history, or the attempt at the alleviation of social problems on treaty-protected lands, or the need for development of a decent tribally oriented economy will not be addressed through the acceptance of the false narrative.

It's not even that any Native protest can impact any of the crises mentioned here or even get a hearing in the enclaves of power. The best we can do is write, speak, and do the scholarly work that will lead us toward a climate in the mainstream of America that acknowledges and defends our presence as First Nations peoples in a democratic America, not one that just makes excuses. It is a political matter that requires a political solution.

The most dangerous thing about all of this is that we will begin to think these white-man wars and atrocities and outrages and contemporary outpourings *are* our Native histories. They are not. They are only the histories of what has happened after our country was invaded, after the North American continent was depopulated and after we became preoccupied with our mere survival. It is recent history, made up to accommodate a white colonial vision. What about the thousands of years before these contemporary musings?

It is dangerous when we give significance to these invasion stories and war atrocities because when that becomes our entire focus, we can never know how rich and important were our legacies before invasion. We can never truly possess a legacy of thousands of years on this land because that history has been overwhelmed by our survival efforts. Our approach to the sun with vistas and plateaus and prairies and rivers shining in the distance and the sheltered positions that helped us know ourselves will be forever missing from our lives.

22

SOME HAVE TRIED TO tell us in Dakota country that there are no important ruins that survive and only a scattering of sacred places, and that our lives have always been remote and unworthy. They say white sculptors from foreign countries can come here and tell us what our leaders like Crazy Horse looked like when in fact no one on this earth knows that because when he was alive he refused to let his likeness be replicated.

All this may mean that we might buy into the belief that our chanting will rise, echo, and fall as our nations did. What chants? Do we know them? Do we remember them? Can we sing new ones? There are literally thousands of them, like this one that I just made up and translated from fragments of more traditional ones:

I pick the fruits from the chokecherry bush
before it doesn't remember who I am
I dig the root of the ti(n)psina
before it moves away from the charred river
and the turtle sinks slowly to entwine the spider web

I was thinking about these things one July day three years ago when I stumbled upon a huge stone edifice of a reptile that lies in the prairie grass on the eastern side of the Missouri River near the trails made by Sitting Bull and Gall and White Ghost as well as thousands of unknown Dakota travelers.

It reminded me that there are literally hundreds of "unknown" places like this. I was told once by an old woman related to my grandfather that there are these sacred places that have not been widely known, and she suggested that it was up to us to revive them for the people. They are the homes of spirits, she said, who have always occupied certain places, and, she warned, they will kill any human beings who come near if they are unfaithful and uncaring.

She was talking about the sacredness of the universe that surrounds us, and she wanted me to know that learning the songs and poems and dances has always been connected to the powerful ways that we dedicate ourselves to the spirits, but even that may not be enough. Custom, she said, requires us to pay strict attention to supernatural beings and take them seriously.

I've never forgotten this old woman. She had no front teeth, so she had a tendency to spit on you as she talked. In that respect she was very like Amos, the old man from Cheyenne River, who talked the same way. He was in some ways offensive but he could cajole you into believing almost anything. One time when our old bitch dog had puppies he talked my sister and me into giving him one of her brood. He was from up north, and as he went down the road toward his home carrying our pup (he walked everywhere), we knew that he and his Minneconjou relatives (they were not Santees) still did the kettle dance in which they sacrificed a dog, and we mourned silently.

We, my older sister and I, tried to avoid both of these old persons but often got caught up in their wily ways. The old woman, whose name I can't remember, was straight and slim and she always wore black, and you could see her stride beside the creek in and out and between the trees. We knew that she was Ihanktowan but knew very little about her otherwise. In those days, the dialects of our language were really noticeable, so as soon as you started to talk people knew which band you were from, a characteristic not so pronounced today. Santees lived up and down that creek in the old days, and they shared those places with many people of our nation.

The day I found the stone edifice that looked like a snake, I stood as if transfixed as the sun got higher in the sky. I wondered if it was one of those places dangerous to humans, like the old woman said. I approached it slowly and carefully.

I felt apprehensive and wondered what rites must be performed there.

No doubt my great imagination was at work, but that was tempered this day by pragmatism. Maybe great ceremonials once took place here, I thought; yet, perhaps, on the other hand, when the spirits witnessed the destruction of the river, they simply left in disgust. Maybe they were gone.

As I walked along in sight of the now channelized Missouri River, the wind rose up, blowing hard and clean. It tore my scarf off, and I had to chase it down. I was alone, on my way to Eagle Butte to get some people to sign a petition about school matters, and I had half a notion to just get in my car and drive on. I didn't feel welcome and knew I should leave.

Yet where the road drops dramatically into a fluvial gorge, I was drawn to the small rise, which is at the mercy of the sun and the wind. I saw that the stones and even the boulders were almost covered by the tall brittle grass.

In retrospect, the rock snake I happened upon that day and others like it, which may be hidden in history, seem to me to be as significant to world knowledge as the Hopi caves and the Inca monuments and the Sistine Chapel and the mosques of Iraq; yet no one knows of them. I happened upon this by mistake not knowing what important role it may have played, not knowing if there were other remains no longer visible. I've never returned but have kept the feeling that forces of the underworld may have assisted the people in worshiping the dead here as well as the living. There is no scientific research that I know of that can tell us anything at all about this. So as I meandered in the tall grass I didn't know where I was or what I was seeing.

Some Dakotas say that there are certain kinds of rocks on the prairie that are struck and formed by lightning, and as I stood in the wind and looked at the troubled sky, I knew that by late afternoon there could well be a thunderstorm that would frighten every creature into its den.

Lightning strikes are powerful and frightening in these scenic places. As I stood there, I looked at the stones in amazement. They formed a very long undulating snake, even had two oval, reddish colored eyes at the elongated head.

I know that stones are considered carriers of knowledge, but I still know little of the sacred world. I am usually a participant in these kinds of things simply at the invitation of relatives. Even when I went to sacred meetings years ago, I had no reason to ask questions about the knowledge of the stones that were handled by the yuwipi man. But I have never really participated wholeheartedly and have avoided being drawn into the unfathomable ancient world, which seems so remote.

The wind tearing at my shirt, I walked around the long body of the snake and stopped counting the rocks when I got to three hundred. Some were very small, others the size of boulders. The body of the rock formation seemed like it might move in a wave-like motion, segments placed so that it seemed crooked and wavy, snake-like. Our word for that is *zu-zu-e-cha*. The shrine was long and almost buried in prairie sand and grass. It had probably been there a couple of hundred years. But it may have been just a temporary thing on some kind of migration route. Who knows how long? Surely, if we remembered the ohunkaka stories of origin, we would know the meaning of this prairie architecture.

I'm sure that no one knows why the snake edifice exists, and I am also sure that no one has investigated this formation to even know that it does exist. Actually, I had happened on it simply because I was on a mission and had driven about twenty or thirty miles north from I-90. I had wanted to get out of my car for a few moments, take a break to have coffee, and look beyond the hills to the west.

I was not on some kind of quest. I was simply lucky that day, a modern visitor who happened upon a remote place doubtless used by ancient priests. My lonesomeness for this vista was what drew me to stop and look about. I get lonesome for this vista when I've been away for a while. I have to stand in the wind and raise my arms over my head and just feel and smell the prairie and the river. My professional life as well as my personal life at this time was taking place a long way from where I stood at that moment, and I was conscious of the vast distance. My work had taken me to Seattle and Phoenix and other distant cities.

I put my thermos on the hood of my Pontiac, poured myself a cup of coffee, and, as I tightened my fingers around the plastic cup, I thought for a moment about how lucky I was, an aging and mature woman now with a good and happy life. I felt the presence of my relatives here.

As I moved, I was astonished at what I was seeing, and I probably saw it only because the wind had opened the tall grass covering. Perhaps, if I were to ask scholars who delve into what we may call ancient mysteries, I might find some further information. Perhaps not. The river has changed since it was channeled by the Corps of Engineers who did their destructive work all the way from North Dakota to Sioux City, Iowa, and beyond. Who knows what roads and rock outcrops and carvings may have been destroyed in the process of dam building?

I stood there a long time before I remembered to rummage around in my car for some tobacco. I left it there and drove slowly away, still mystified by what I had seen.

The hydropower dams had flooded the banks and thousands of acres of the reservations as well as my father's small ranching place, where he and I often rode into the bend of the river landscape to find wild turnips. We paid attention to the focus of the sun and leaned over our saddles and looked everywhere for the pale blue flower of the Indian turnip, ti(n)psina, usually found in groups of three.

When we couldn't find them in the usual places my father said, "Everything has moved, daughter . . . ti(n)psina . . . the little crea-tures . . . even the rattlers. Everything is gone someplace else now, where it is more comfortable."

Everything changes, but one thing we can say about the snake edi-fice: it very likely will not move. It may be there hundreds of years from now, so that other lucky passersby can come upon it and marvel.

23

BY THE CONVENTIONAL STANDARDS of the academic world, in which I have spent many decades, there is always the notion that you can know for certain the answers to profound questions. That is the function of religion too. Maybe, though, it is the function of Native religions to tell you that you cannot know, and that is even more valuable a lesson.

More probably, to know the answers to questions is the function of *law*, man-made law, that is, and science. These are the disciplines of legal studies in which the ideals of the educated class are buried beneath the years. Some tell us that America counts on three of its foremost traits for safety and success. These three traits are competition, science, and law.

It is here in these learned sanctuaries we are taught that we are to thrive, feel safe, and find solace in an ever-expanding universe. I've lived long enough now to know that sometimes, especially when we are young, the unexplainable passions that come from living a tribal life are strangely altered, and they have nothing to do with America's goals. They often lead to those unsafe places at any speed.

As an American Indian, I am sure to say (however reluctantly), that there are few places for me to feel safe. It is possible that those unexplainable passions of tribal life can be not just altered but crowded out by the unnoticed busyness of daily living. The tribal passion or knowledge tells you that you are a remnant of the living earth but it all can be replaced so that you are no longer dependent on the earth as other creatures are. That may be the shame of modern life.

That feeling of safety in the earth's arms, then, is replaced simply by keeping the arms of your human relatives around you, wherever you are. Place and ritualistic attention are changeable things. No longer do you go to the sweat lodge for comfort any more, just as Catholics no longer go to the church for solace. You go where your human relatives are.

In my case, I was lucky to have been born and to have lived in a country where my relatives lived, along the dense trees at Fort Thompson and Big Bend, which meant that as a child I could find safety there. There were few places to feel safe in those days, but I remember with great fondness the little village (before it was flooded by power dams in the Missouri), where I often stayed with relatives who worked for the federal government. The reality of that life, I will be the first to admit, was hard: poverty; the human frailties that make family life chaotic, selfishness and conflicts; lack of decent housing and the unpredictable weather of the Northern Plains.

It was a place that my grandparents knew as a place guarded by soldiers and police and bureaucrats of the federal government in a time when Indian scalps brought two hundred dollars each, but it seemed to the coming generations of children with loving parents that it was a place of safety. It was still a place of the tiospaye for many of us, and we would bring our own overnight blankets and sleep on the floor of the home of my Auntie Martha, who knew how to be a good relative. The men and boys slept outside, smoking and talking into the early hours. Auntie had a piano in her house (probably the only one on the whole reservation), and if we got there early enough she would play tunes she had learned at the boarding school in Rapid City when she was young.

Fort Thompson was the seat of bureaucratic government as early as 1863, named after a military overlord and peopled by many of the descendants of the survivors of Little Crow War in Minnesota. The village that it became and that I knew as a child is now completely under water, as is the huge IHS hospital that tended to the health needs of several tribes, sacrificed for hydropower.

177

A new little village now stands up on the bluff away from the water, complete with tribal housing and a gambling casino among the federal office buildings, gas stations, and motels. All that sounds easy, but it wasn't. Removals and other kinds of destructions concerning the river development are part of the past.

Auntie Martha knew how to read music and sometimes referred to her Scott Joplin sheet music. She taught me how to read music, but I did not have much devotion and rarely practiced. Today I can play such piano tunes as "Smoke Gets in Your Eyes" and "Bridge over Troubled Water." Auntie played the piano for a very popular little tribal dance band called the Red Ramblers in the 1940s. It was named for Red Big Eagle, who played the cornet and sang in a corny mimic of Louis Armstrong. His voice was loud and his face was red, and I thought of him as a buffoon. His son later became an important tribal council chairman.

My father, who had attended that same boarding school, played melody sax, and with Elgie Jenese on clarinet and Uncle Amos on banjo gave a raucous rendition of what my grandmother called white-man music far into the night on weekends. They all had gone to boarding schools where white-man music was part of the curriculum, as were the "arts" of learning to milk cows and speaking English.

In the summertime there would usually be a fire outside on the grounds of our auntie's place, where the boys and men slept. People were quiet on the floor inside, and one of the old women would sometimes start to sing a soft song and I would weep silently for no reason at all. The weeping was just the feeling of being safe and cared for and among those you loved. Whatever it was I didn't know made questioning okay there in those warm corners next to others. If I was seeking to ask myself big questions about how to shape some kind of order in my world, those imaginations and worries were all dismissed in this place.

Of all the places I've known, this was where I knew we were safe. I can hardly remember that feeling now.

Since that forgotten time, I've quit the kind of appreciative sadness that I think I was born with, the kind of emotional mood that made me give into some kind of aesthetic urge. I wrote things down very early, as soon as I learned to read and write English. That meant I wanted to spend a lot of time by myself.

My father was a horseman and rancher, and all of us in the family knew he liked to live by himself. He was, I think, the only one who really understood that urge toward isolation. He recognized it in me, his youngest child. When we would talk together, which was a rare occasion, he would say, "Daughter . . . you need to be alone. You were *born* too old for this world. You need to be alone," and then he would laugh out loud, like it was some kind of joke.

As a child, the loss of the sun at the end of the day seemed to be a loss that was unbearably sad to me. I cried a lot out of this feeling. Some things are brought on in the lives of children by an unknown and unfathomable unease that simply has no reason, a function of temperament, perhaps. There is no rationale for this but I have kept these childhood ways in my memory for many years.

To show just how long-lasting such traits are, I remember this strange encounter: As an adult driving home from Washington State to see my aging parents, I was walking down the street in Fort Pierre where I had stopped to get a tire fixed. An old friend I hadn't seen in ten years, a guy I'd gone to mission school with but who on this Sunday morning was coming down from his particular reverence, hollered at me in English from across the street like I had just seen him last week. "Ho, 'Lizbeth . . . are you sober?"

I didn't answer him, just waved.

Then as an afterthought, he shouted, "Hey, did you ever stop crying?"

He meandered on down the street, and I went to check on my car at the garage. Bewildered and a little insulted, I thought, is that my legacy, a nine-year-old kid just trying to grow up? Is that what he remembers about me? The truth is I was rarely alone, and I can't remember ever being depressed. After I became an adult, I recognized this feeling as having something to do with the utter solace of familiar places and things like the touch of the wind or the smell of the grass or the heat of the relentless sun. Like my father I have always wanted to be alone and nurture those feelings of inevitable prairie journeys to think my own thoughts. In some odd way, those feelings that even today I can't describe give me intense feelings of wellbeing. There is something exquisite about private thoughts and precious times to be shared with no one.

My mother was an independent woman who tried to point me in more functional directions, saying "happiness is where you find it. Be happy, child." She would admonish me, not really understanding that I was, in truth, a happy and contented child. I think she thought I was "disturbed," and later on when I was in college and read some educational psychology books, I kind of know what she might have thought. "Disturbed" children are often those who are just misunderstood. They are often "crybabies." And loners. In my mind I was neither, though others may have thought so.

I remember my mother singing old songs from the 1920s. She was cheerful, always had a smile on her face and a positive and sunshiny presence, which meant that she did not like my more ponderous demeanor mostly because she didn't understand it.

Real sadness, though, grief born of tragedy, is a different thing.

When my older brother quit high school and left for the navy six days after Pearl Harbor, it wasn't in our thoughts that he would never return, and we really didn't know real sadness or profound grief as a family until that happened. When he didn't make it home, it changed all our lives.

Vic had lived with white folks from the time he was born until he was nine, so he didn't know the Dakota language and always talked English. He was tall and handsome, the horseshoe-playing champion of Crow Creek at the age of twelve, and he could break any horse to ride in a few hours. He was a great athlete, a state champion pole vaulter, and later, in the navy, when he was stationed in Nevada, he became a golf pro.

We younger siblings used to walk to a country school a few miles from our place, and before he left for the navy he would always tempt me, the youngest, to ride with him on one of the so-called saddle broncs he was always in the process of training. "Come on!" he'd challenge. "I'll bet you're afraid." He and Joe Blacksmith prided themselves on being the oldest kids at the reservation school and the best riders anywhere around.

The truth is I was afraid of horses. His horses were always prancing and rearing up. Vic thought he was the Cisco Kid which was the stereotypical character in his favorite movie. Or maybe he was trying to be Zorro!

He and Joe Blacksmith were not very attentive at this country school on the Crow Creek, very fun loving, and I missed them both when they went off to the federal boarding school at the agency for high school. That federally run high school boarding place for teenagers is long gone, too, as are so many of the places of the community. Joe would come over to our place every Sunday because my grandparents who lived nearer the creek were there, and my mother would butcher some chickens for a fine table feast we shared with him and many others from the community. It was a Sunday thing because very few of us in our Santee family went to the churches where others gathered regularly after the services. Sometimes Joe would bring over a dead porcupine (roadkill) for my grandmother, who would spend hours harvesting the quills and the long hair for her quillwork and beadwork.

While some people say that the Sioux cuisine included porcupine, that wasn't Joe's intent. In those days the Santees and the Yanktons never ate porcupine. They called him pahin and often just chased him away when they saw him. If he was slow enough they would throw a blanket over him to catch his quills.

While Vic was at the federal boarding school during the year, he spent his summers at the mission school in Stephan, where the students had access to a herd of cows to learn how to milk and a pasture full of horses. Once when my sister and I lived at my father's place, we had baked a cake because we were home alone and had nothing to do. We looked out the window and saw Vic and six or seven of his buddies ride in on beautiful bay horses like something out of a John Wayne movie, a distance of about thirteen miles from the school, dust and hoofs flying. The riders and our brother came in the kitchen and without our permission or invitation wolfed down our three-layered pink cake. They rode off as quickly as they had come, hollering "Pedamayea" to the wind.

We were angry. About seven or eight years old, we'd had a big struggle to make the cake from scratch, and we were not happy to have it so quickly and unceremoniously gobbled up. We griped at him when we saw him about a week later. It was not one of our favorite memories.

Even before Vic came home to live with us, the family would go to Lower Brulé across the river where there was a huge racetrack, and the old men with long, braided hair who still wore moccasins would participate in what they called "sulkey races." They had fine-looking chariots and bred the finest horses. They even went to the state fairs with their horses to compete with the white men from what my father called "the settlements."

It was expected that my brother (Chunskay, we called him) would come home from the navy and join the community, but he didn't. Returning from Japan, he was set to do embassy duty in England, but the night before he left, after having survived many sea battles of World War II and Korea, he was killed in an auto accident driving out of El Toro marine base in California.

There was a four-day wake, the saddest time our family ever witnessed. Relatives we hadn't seen for years came from everywhere. The drum group from the agency, many of them his old school friends, sang those old warrior songs, and of course someone from his outfit who had accompanied his body home from his base in California played "Taps." I don't know which was the more wrenching ritual, "Taps" or old warrior songs. My father drank heavily for years after this death in the family.

A modern visitor to any Sioux reservation is always struck by the enigma of tribal military service, illustrated by the careful attention to the military dedication and consciousness of the Oyate who, more than any other peoples in the United States, would be thought by outsiders to find the U.S. military loathsome.

That is not true in the Sioux Tribe. There are many unanswered questions about how the indigenous people defend their homelands, how the defensive network of military service of past generations brings pride and security to a beleaguered people. My brother was a young man who had male relatives who had fought at the Little Big Horn. His grandmother had been a child witness to the U.S. military's hanging of thirty-eight Dakotas at New Ulm after the Little Crow War in Minnesota. His father and uncles on both sides of the family had done military service, and communal veterans' services were commonplace. Every community gathering started with an honoring of the flags. And still does. This kind of dedication has never been explained to anyone's satisfaction. Other tribes in the United States do not share this history.

A Cherokee professor of Native studies I've known for a while wrote a book in 1996 called *Strong Hearts, Wounded Souls*, and it includes a quote from a Seneca vet of the Vietnam War that wrenches your soul: "When I got to the bush my platoon sergeant tells me and the guys I came in with that we were surrounded. He said: 'The gooks are all out there and we're here. This is Fort Apache, boys, and out there is Indian Country.' Can you fuckin' believe that! To me? I should have shot him right then and there. Made me wonder who the real enemy was." As a writer, I would never in a million years attempt to go into the *theory* of "the warrior society" because it is just too absurd and ubiquitous to me to try to refute.

Another theory is the poverty theory—that idleness and "lack of opportunity" on the reservations pushes young men and women into the military. When my youngest takoja joined the marines in 2005 and went to Fallujah, Iraq, I wept for days, months, years. He was nineteen and I was over seventy years of age, and I thought: what does he know? Once, when he first came home, he told me he does not want to carry the U.S. flag nor the tribal flag in the honoring ceremonials, nor any flag of any country.

Whatever I say will not give spirit to any of the actions of thousands of indigenous people from tribe to tribe who have given their youth and sometimes their lives for the landscape of this sanctuary called the homelands. The movements of the sun and the human aspiration for earth's physical forces will have to be translated by each of them.

This digression into the dilemmas of a once-traditional family now almost entirely disintegrated through the passage of time is not my style, and it doesn't fit the notions with which I began this memoir, that is, that of the intellectual and political priorities or the critical forces of this life I am trying to describe. Yet I include these unforgettable episodes to give substance to the question of how one goes about choosing one's life's work. We all must do that at any age. The choice of a military life in America, a country at war for the most of the twentieth century, is unfathomable to me.

24

Keyapi

THE "CHOOSING" OF MY work to become a political writer and teacher seems to be even stranger and in some ways even more randomly accidental than most of the events of my long life.

One requirement, though, for this course of events is that a political person must have three things going: a fascination with both language and ideas, inborn intellectual curiosity, and opportunity. It's not a simple thing, starting with no real sense of anything except the need to be left alone without uncommon pressure, which, in spite of what the modernists say, is a good thing for a writer.

There was no place for me to go to acquire skills in teaching or learning or critical thinking or paying attention to aspirations toward political will and intelligence, all major traits of most serious political writers. The subjugated regions where most Indians lived in my early days did not allow us the luxury of worrying about the national and international movements embodying such esoteric matters above and beyond mere survival. Yet these kinds of movements were taking place all over the world, and they would eventually catch up with me on Indian reservations in South Dakota.

There was little possibility of meeting or knowing successful writers to get an understanding of the writer's way of life. To say we had no communications systems during my growing-up years is an understatement. We had no electricity. Telephone. Television. Radio. It sounds comical to say that I remember walking two miles with my father and one of my cousins to a white neighbor's house after dark in the dead of winter when they wanted to listen to a Joe Louis fight on the radio. Wouldn't you think we would have at least had a battery-run radio? The truth is, in my grandmother's house, where I spent early years, there was no clock, no timepiece of any kind. I should probably say something more about this because it went beyond poverty. It was preference, especially for that grandmother.

In the midst of such poverty and preference it hardly seems possible that one would know anything about indigenous and peasant organizations or popular front organizations or political enclaves that might be going on in other parts of the county as the struggle for freedom against colonial rule was heating up in the twentieth century. Oddly, there was always Indian talk, vague and muted, suspicious and risky, especially among the men in my family.

In 1943 or 1944, just during the war, my father went to Washington DC to become a charter member of the National Congress of American Indians as a delegate of the Santee Oyate and the Crow Creek Sioux Tribe. It may have been in Denver; I can't remember for certain. He had been a citizen of the United States for a few decades and was trying to step into two different political worlds. Many in his generation and his father's had already worked toward understanding the legal and political theft of lands, especially the sacred Black Hills land theft. The repression of American Indians and the routine forms of colonization we knew were so complete that it wasn't until about 1950 that Indians from the South Dakota reservations really became engaged in particular experiences of how to achieve power and overcome the powerlessness of generations of inhumane treatment we knew.

Liberation theology may have been going on elsewhere, but reservation life in the Midwest as I knew it was devoid of any such overt struggle for a long time. Colonization is not just the taking-over of land and resources and initiating a repressive regime for reasons of control and economics. It is also the overt humiliation suffered by powerless people that comes with the poverty of chance and potential. When a great and greedy power comes in, carves up the landscape, and kills and relocates inhabitants, which is what happened to tribal people, there is little possibility for escape.

After I passed thirty years of age, after college, after a bad marriage and a commitment to parenthood, an insurgency of self-knowledge went on for me. It was not so much a choice as it was simply a desperate need to get some control over the situations that had always been repressive. And it was a growing-up period. Life was hard and I grew up. By this time I had done massive amounts of reading, a life-saving activity that fed my soul. It was a catching-up remedy for an inferior educational experience.

In these times and against all odds, an irresistible message was being received in Indian Country that we as Indians should learn to speak for ourselves. There was a considerable amount of material being published about Indians in those years from 1960 through the end of the century because of the larger community's recognition of a largely unspoken racial and political history. Many of us were reading and acknowledging its access.

Eventually, as Indians, we joined in the writing for ourselves.

There was a strategic shift in Indian America during those decades, and the shift entailed *identifying the false story* that quickly became the defensive mechanism we all found useful. For a kid who only saw cowboys and Indians movies at a local theater in an adjoining town and mindlessly cheered for the cowboys to win, I finally became an adult and began to see the false story. Indians getting shot out of the saddle by John Wayne, the white cowboy and the military guy in his blue uniform, has been an enduring myth in America. It has been difficult for America to give it up. Even many years later, Kevin Costner took global prizes for telling the story of the disappearing Indian and the White Guy owning the world.

For a very long time, we had developed few skills for analysis and writing. In the shift away from just squirming in discomfort in hearing these false stories, we all had to learn that we as Indians and as worthy members of the human race would no longer stand at the door of the little house on the prairie asking for food.

I quickly became enamored of conceptualizing the false story as a real enemy, which was a useful tactic because it could unite all tribal people in the West. The response to this freedom for many of us was not to overthrow the government, which so many whites feared when the American Indian Movement came on the scene and so many radicals talked about.

The response was simply to identify the false story at long last. For many Indians who were not going to go into the streets to protest, that seemed to be enough. We can argue about whether or not it was enough because, as an observer as well as a participant, I am not sure that it was.

Eventually, though, this identification of the false story became a broad academic movement and some called it a renaissance. *The Indian Historian*, edited by Jeannette Henry and published by the American Indian Historical Society out of San Francisco, was organized by Native scholars and sympathetic historians and anthropologists in the late 1960s. It was copyrighted by 1971 and became a guidebook for academia.

It became notable as the interpretive and historical text that greatly stimulated scholarship and writing and research, publishing some of the best prose and poetry of any era. One of the first pieces I remember reading was "White-Created Myths about the Native Americans" by Joe S. Sando, which very simply demanded that the truth be told. This kind of thing eventually led, decades later, to such collections as diverse as *American Indian Sovereignty and the Supreme Court* by David Wilkins and *Indian Historians Write Back* by Susan Miller and James Riding In, all cheered on by the early essays of Vine Deloria starting with *Custer Died For Your Sins*.

In the fall of 1980, I visited the offices of that publication with Dr. Bea Medicine, anthropologist and scholar born and raised at Wakpala, South Dakota. The estate of *The Indian Historian* was situated on a hill in San Francisco where the magazine originated and where Jeannette lived with her husband, Rupert Costo, for many years; Bea knew Jeannette as a personal friend from the days when she taught in the Bay Area.

My visit there took place after Rupert's death, and Jeannette was now a wraith-like old woman, weighing barely ninety pounds. She was almost unable to walk but led us up the lush, carpeted stairway to Rupert's bedroom that she left as he had left it on the night he died, bed unmade and a glass of water at the night table. His reading text was left open to the last page he had read before his death. This place was almost a shrine by this time; the tragedy is that the whole publishing enterprise that had been so important to their entire lives sort of withered as Rupert and Jeannette aged, and it was no longer the beacon of indigenous studies that could have continued into the present time if only appropriate passage into the future had been planned. The Rupert Costo academic chair in American Indian history, however, has been an enduring repository of scholarship at the University of California, and some offshoots of this scholarship have survived at nearby universities and repositories.

After our visit with Jeannette, we were touched by the reverence of her dedicated life. We drove north out of the city almost in silence. We went to Washington State, where I lived sometimes in a log house on the Columbia River with CJ. Because it was Bea's birthday, and because of the thoughts concerning the aging of two important scholars whose work was now in danger of falling into near obscurity, we fell to joking about how it is to get old. And irrelevant.

Later, my husband, CJ, who really got along with Bea better than I did and always had a sharper sense of humor than I did, met us in the living room and greeted us by calling us "world travelers" and "jet-setters."

Then he turned to Bea and said, "I have a gift for you . . . in fact, two gifts."

"Oh." We both perked up.

"You can take your pick."

He went to the closet and brought out two packages.

"One is a cane," he said, displaying a beautifully beaded walking stick, avoiding any more old-age jokes, "and the other is a fifth of scotch," holding a brown sack at arm's length.

I'll leave it up to those who knew her well to tell you which gift she chose.

Many of us have agreed that getting old is a privilege, but one of the things I've noticed about early academics in our field, like the Costos, is that we do not mentor very well, which means we do not take on acolytes and force them into our molds, that much fame and excellence dies when the scholar leaves his or her post. Costo's legacy is a rarity.

There are few great monuments to the intellectual giants who have told our lives throughout the twentieth century. We build statues to the eighteenth-century Winnebago Clan leaders, for example, on the reservation tourist circle, but the greatness of Black Elk is not enshrined in a statue or a building or a monument at the University of Nebraska, where his white interpreter, John B. Neihardt, has a classroom building and a museum dedicated in his own name. Settlers and invaders know how to do these things but indigenous peoples are often the forgotten few. Just recently, though, places in the Black Hills have been renamed, and new inscriptions have appeared on campus buildings in recognition of Indian notables.

As far as I know, there is still no huge and official Vine Deloria Jr. Library anywhere in the West; yet he was among those who was truly a heroic figure and certainly was a main intellectual influence in the renaissance classics. Many of the people we've known as Native scholars have interpreted events that reflect the concerns of what is now called liberation theology. Many of them, like Vine and Bea and the Costos and hundreds more I cannot name here, have changed the Indian world. Yet there is remarkably little attention paid to the scholar class.

Perhaps it is because the matters they spoke of and wrote about are still a potent threat to the colonial structures that hold lands and resources and lives in bondage, to say nothing of the intellectual theft or denigration that thwarts the recognition of Indian works.

We don't even pay much attention to great collections of essays presented by Native scholars such as *Crossbloods: Bone Courts, Bingo, and Other Reports* (University of Minnesota Press, 1976), which is really an important journalistic work written by Gerald Vizenor, who calls himself a mixed-blood. It's a work that gives us in present time a view of the past. Journalism, after all, provides the place where the earliest stories are written down and should take a prominent place in archival materials.

Thinking of this and recognizing that even though there may be some controversy about what may define a crossblood or a mixed-blood, I remind myself when I look at the work of someone like Vizenor and countless others that we don't have to explore Kant, Hegel, and Marx to know what society's encroachment on Native peoples has wrought. We have our own neglected texts, often inaccessible for various reasons.

Literary studies led the way. During the early period, the journal I was editing, the *Wicazo Śa Review*, published a piece by a brilliant white critic named Dr. Lawrence J. Evers, originally from Nebraska, a piece that helped to define the scholarly work that was being done by poets and novelists and that was essential to the stable future of the emerging discipline of Indian literary studies. Evers's essay was called "The Killing of a New Mexican State Trooper: Ways of Telling a Historical Event," a fascinating examination of two short stories: one "Tony's Story" by Leslie Silko and "The Killing of a State Cop" by Simon Ortiz.

I heard Evers read the paper in a full classroom at a Rocky Mountain Modern Language Association meeting in Santa Fe, New Mexico, in 1976, and I wanted to talk to him, but since I was not yet in the circle of scholar-writers doing this work, I did not approach him. Some at that time were suggesting that the murders in these events exemplified Truman Capote's *In Cold Blood* kind of senseless killing, and that may have been one of the reasons for popular scholarly interest. The Native story went quickly by the wayside. And Capote became a star.

What the lit-crit piece really did in terms of indigenous theories of literature as well as history was to examine the threatening presences known in the Indian world that are sometimes mythic and sometimes real but always present in the context of land and thousands of years of indigenous inhabitation. It was about murder and the spirits on the "other side" known to the Tewa peoples. This critical essay was a stunning step forward for many of us who were even then reluctantly visiting bookstores where various kinds of trash called "Indian works" still held sway—awful writings done by non-Native scholars who knew nothing about Indians except to reiterate the ever-present examination of the deficit model of poverty and chaos.

Readers flocked to such places as a wonderfully contemporary bookstore I knew on the streets of Santa Fe, for example, where a raucous display of *The Death of the Great Spirit: An Elegy for the American Indian* could be had at a cut-rate price. It was a messy, trashy, wailing, feeble attempt by Earl Shorris whose aim was to talk about the failure of contemporary Indian life and history. It was being touted by Simon and Schuster as "remarkable" and "groundbreaking." An elegy, as you probably know, is a mournful piece, composed to lament the dead. As I paged through it, I wondered about the incredible gall it takes to declare an entire population of a country dead; yet American writers have done it over and over again. And unknowledgeable readers are entranced.

While Evers's work was evidence that the dual nature of Indian lives still rested in the mountains and rocks and the enigmatic past, Shorris apparently was, at that moment, leaving his boring white-man life in San Francisco, where he was working as a journalist-novelist (which is notable in Indian literary circles as the most deadly combination of writerly intentions), to visit Sioux Indian reservations in

South Dakota and write down his observations and interviews. He was said to be talking to Sitting Bull's "scattered spiritual descendants" to say that "real" Indians are dead and they have lost a three-hundred-year war with people who have "loved them to death" with Christian kindness. This weird overestimation and idealization of the ugliest history of indigenous-colonial conflict anywhere in the world is very popular in some circles.

The Shorris work is a scurrilous book. It is a self-indulgent ventilation from a white man who, apparently, was eager to cash in on all of the other scurrilous books written during this time by strange men and women who flocked to Indian reservations for some reason of unaccountable curiosity. It might have made it as a short, mean, racist commentary in a letter to the editor in some regional newspaper to satisfy other unthinking white folks, but as a revealing portrait of imaginative or historical literature it fails. It nonetheless found a publisher, one of the stalwarts.

It's safe to say, probably, that few are exempted from reading these kinds of books behind the headlines of whatever mainstream America is thinking about at any given time. Indians find these works at every bookstore! They have been extremely popular with the non-Indian American public, something like the dime novels of the late 1800s.

Shorris did his homework as an interviewer. Everybody shows up in the pages of this white man's version of the false story: Frank Takes the Gun, Carlos Castaneda, Fools Crow, Descartes, Rousseau, Andrew Jackson, Lehman Brightman, Emory Sekaquaptewa, Peter Nuvamsa, Calvin Jumping Bull, several people named Red Cloud, Gerald One Feather, the daughter of Silas Afraid of Enemy, Lois Taylor and husband Dennis, an Indian woman who says she fought with the Israelis and Mad Bear Anderson, Richard Oakes and Stella Leech, Grace Thorpe, even Jack Forbes. John Trudell, the guitarist who says he is Santee, appears in the final pages, and he is asked to sing something by Bob Dylan. These people make up a motley crew who show up on every page almost in that order. It's not that these people aren't real. They are real, and I have known many of them. It's that the story told is a testament to the failure of collective ideals that are tribal in nature and, more specifically, pan-tribal in nature, of a people the white-man narrator holds in great contempt.

What's new about that, you ask? What's new is that between Shorris's talky, self-satisfied observations and silly musings packed with just plain meanness, the miracle of the uprisings that were going on in the 1970s when this book was written lacks any understanding of the nature of indigenousness implicit in culture and political experience. And it overshadows some very fine work being done by Native writers who were trying to find what might be called the contemporary Indian voice. Sometimes the frames drawn by white Americans who write about what happens to colonized peoples around a struggling but powerful collective called tribalism is no help at all if what we want to do is grapple with the dilemmas and criminal nature of Indian-white history of colonization. Shorris, a third-rate writer at best, surely could have striven to do something other than call people names in order to humiliate them.

All of this is, quite naturally, a function of coloniality that has many descriptions. It appears that colonized peoples like American Indians cannot just move into modernity, claiming their own place, actively taking up their own histories without white observers conjuring up false images. I suppose it is always the case that alliances have to be made across a colonial divide but only if it is possible to do so without making enormous concessions to the colonist's needs.

Such writing as Shorris's, scholars would say, is tethered to the first world, to capitalism, the thinking that defines his world so that he can on the one hand hold Natives in contempt while on the other hand claim love and pity for them. This is America's sickness. This dilemma accounts for what was going on with average Americans in the 1970s and for two decades hence who wanted to dominate Indians yet do it in an embracing way. They continued to defend an imperialistic history so that their occupation of stolen land could be legitimized and the need not accept any blame put on them by Indians.

A certain kind of nationalism is absolutely essential to indigenous populations all around the world if there is to be a challenge to the process of colonization, yet the erasing of the contract with Native nations in America is done only through a process of collective memory erasure. Rarely is it done officially anywhere in the world without a war or a revolution.

When speakers and writers for AIM came along, suspicion and an exaggerated sense of one's own importance, including a sense of outraged victimhood, characterized much of the dialogue by men like Dennis Banks and Russell Means, who captured and expressed the emotional fury of the legitimate but tacit rage in all of us. They helped us to recognize that there was nothing random about the political cruelties of being an indigenous person in America.

They accused everyone of something. Toward us, their fellow Indians who were scholars, the accusation of not being true to the agony of personal histories and traumas was fierce. For example, our academic interest in trying to translate the Major Crimes Act, which took away our law and order and made us invisible, or the accommodation with the Allotment Act, etching our loss of place and language, they told us, would have to be denounced in the streets as false. The leaders of the American Indian Movement inspired some of us to set our sights on the pursuit of the deliberate horrors of colonialism with the idea of understanding the crimes of ideological politics in America, but they wanted to do it more publicly than some.

When I met Banks at a seminar at Augustana College in Sioux Falls, South Dakota, when I was in graduate school, he had little interest in the scholarly work being done. This was not the first time I'd met him, as he had been around the Midwest when he worked for the Four M Company out of Minneapolis, with short hair, blue suit and tie, talking to teachers and school officials about the sad state of affairs in teaching Indian history and tribal politics. I was impressed with the change in him.

Now he was an Ojibwe man with long braids, beaded leather vest, and a white man's name. In English, still his only language, he was eloquent, persuasive, charismatic. His judgment and rationale for the movement toward decolonization that he led was a call to war for him, and he was convincing. The American Indian Movement described the realities of the situation of Native America in graphic ways, and we knew he was right every time we heard him speak. As a talented orator, he had little respect for the written word.

During the seminar, Gene Sekaquaptewa from Hopi got up to speak about the importance of education and history and said, "I'm the only real Indian here, my name is as old as the earth," and he pronounced it for us and spelled it out. He said a few words in his Native language. "Some of you don't even have your own names," he said, just minutes before someone in the back of the room dragged out a sack of apples (red on the outside, white on the inside) and hurled them at the speaker who, if he hadn't ducked, would have been beaned right in the middle of his forehead.

This kind of accusation, while probably true historically speaking, only served to divide the listeners, yet it held sway in many circumstances because it was felt then and since that there had been many instances in history when Native people simply gave up their legacies and joined the assimilated throngs of America. The brutal confrontation of living through what was thought by some to be the end of a civilization was too much for many throughout history, and they concluded that there would never be any trust again in the survival of tribalism. That view accounted for an assimilation of the people that found life too difficult.

Native groups still tended to draw back from the revolutionary trend, failing to formulate a language that would satisfy sensitivities. Many indoctrinated through the muted language ordinarily used in tribal sectors were appalled and embarrassed by the virulent articulation of differing views which seemed to encourage us to wage out-and-out war, and many weren't ready for that! This meant that the fiercest venom came from those who had nothing to lose.

The truth is many gains were made because of those people who had nothing to lose. They had not sold out as some had. Yet, how to protect the interests of those who had not sold out was a visible issue. Ordinary citizens, relatives who worked for the BIA at the agency like my Uncle Dan, the schoolchildren of our neighbors who had allowed themselves to be captured by the priests, the reasonably successful Native ranchers and horsemen who still possessed Indian lands doled out by the illegal Allotment Act of the 1800s and held "in trust" now feared the loss of it. Fear of losing the trust responsibility of the federal government inherent in treaty status was voiced by the conservatives.

When Banks in a later tribal meeting at Fort Thompson verbally attacked people in the reservation audience as "half-breeds" and "sell-outs," indicating they were part of the problem not the solution, many of my conservative relatives drew away. The death of tribal cohesiveness happened when too much power went to the celebrity leadership because many in his audience who came from long-suppressed communities had little time for education and preparedness.

The concept of a defensive war waged by people far from power enclaves against poverty and oppression as well as the anti-Indian or racist legislation of the U.S. Congress was seen by most in those days as a futile attempt to dismantle the authority of colonialism. In this process, there is no doubt that paranoia and the notion that "victims" of incredibly powerful outside forces forced people to think there were no alternatives. What is distinctive about the Native or tribal leadership during those times is that there was no notion that there were two sides to this history. There was no "either/or" in the discussion of what the alternatives might be. To say in those days that Indians were benefiting from "liberalism" or "diversity" was unacceptable. Yet the future was uncertain.

Leadership thirty years later seems to suggest the opposite, that in fact we can continue to search for something called universalism. The argument continues. Benefiting more in a relative way than we did in the past seems okay to some, flimsy and unworkable to others. The formation of an Indian policy that retains its racist stance does not mean that we are benefiting, say the dissenters.

Those who recall treaty rights and the sovereign rights to nationalistic trends believe in the need to articulate a policy that is steeped in a tribal vision, not in some kind of semicolonial policy that continues to hold hostages through land and resource management by the federal government. When I look back to the 1970s, the time seems like a pivotal moment in which American Indians were to decide on their visions of the future.

Native people were still in the midst of responding to the termination and relocation laws written by Congress, which were designed to do one or two things: first, to remove Indian peoples from their lands (a state-inspired tactic because Indian lands are not taxable by state governments) and second, to assist Indians in "joining the mainstream of America," a place where we all drown (touted as an idea to seek justice promoted by those in America who claimed these were Christian principles).

My favorite cousin, Jack, with whom I had grown up at my grandmother's house when his parents divorced, was twenty-four years old in these times fraught with change and was excited to follow in the footsteps of our uncle Lawrence, a graduate of Haskell Indian School, by relocating to Minneapolis. It is amazing how quickly Indians respond to the latest tactic promoted by the feds: relocation, casinos, and all the rest. Jack ended up getting stabbed almost to death on Franklin Avenue by a black man who had also, as it happened, relocated to Minneapolis from Mississippi. This was the beginning of the rise of the American Indian Movement in urban America.

After Jack's recovery, he joined the navy for six years and disappeared into the mainstream, living his isolated adult life for a long time in California. The last time I talked to him (he was then older than eighty-five), I tried to talk Indian, but he said he had forgotten our language and refused to join in. Life on the streets for Indians during those relocation years was often not worth celebrating if what we wanted was to keep hope alive.

In many ways, that cousin was the model for a character I imagined for one of the first and the last pieces of fiction I have tried to write. His fictional name is Philip Big Pipe, and, like all of my characters, he exhibits my own study in some kind of skepticism. He is a figure etched in loss, caught up in the results of a destructive movement yet filled with melancholic optimism. Philip appears in the earliest story I published, which was called *From the River's Edge* (Arcade, 1991), as a fleeting character in that long fiction about the flooding of 550 square miles of Indian land. He appears in the final pages of that novella, participating in a sweat lodge ceremony with the main character, his uncle John Tatekeya.

I didn't want the later fictional character Philip to disappear into the mainstream as my cousin Jack had done in our real lives, so I tried to write him into being in my longing for the real life I imagined to be our communal tribal life. The title of that story is That Guy Wolf Dancing (Michigan State University Press, 2014). I wrote much of it when I was living by myself in an apartment in Mesa, Arizona, and teaching at ASU. A decade between those two efforts at writing fiction perhaps tells you a lot about my highly unsuitable and self-destroying career as a fiction writer. The lapse of years between the publication is in no way in variance with my philosophy concerning indigenous life as I know it, and many of my readers have remarked about how the stories are regarded as a continuum. In other words, writers often write the same old story and carry on their same old private obsessions.

The reason to bring it up is that it may suggest this: the difference between a midwestern voice, and an Indian voice, which writers have to contend with when their work becomes public, is too broad a span for characters and events to find contemporaries with whom one can find inspiration.

Indeed, Gregory L. Morris, a professor of American Literature at Penn State University, Erie, tried to include my work in a *Voices of the New West* volume in 1994, saying that there is a "less coherent" voice coming from today's writers, which means, one supposes, that there is an eclectic body of work out there called "western." Thus, he tries to include me with Montana writers Ivan Doig and Gretel Ehrlich and others. It's not that I don't appreciate the effort, it's just that as an Indian writer who has written extensively about land theft issues vis-à-vis the tribes, who is now expected to share an impressive literary culture with those whose folks stole the land, for me the whole literary enterprise obscures the experience. A midwestern voice is one that explores a specific geography and its people in the middle lands of a place of infinite diversity, a place of settler populations as well as indigenous peoples, and many who have read my stories want to believe I am a midwestern voice.

As further verification of that notion, I participated in a statewide endowment project called Prairie Voices, subtitled Reflections on the Land and Its People. I drove to libraries in Rapid City, Pierre, Aberdeen, and Brookings during a four-month period and read from some of my work. After one reading, which expressed the legal conundrum called the Black Hills land theft case, a young student in the front row asked in all innocence the fateful question: "Why do you want your land back?"

It was after that experience my thoughts reflected the futility of my life's work as a writer. The sky had turned dark as I walked to my car. I drove home in a dismal rain thinking, *what's the point of all this writing and talking that I do?* I'm past middle age now and coming to the realization that we might never recover from the racial upheaval caused by the European "discovery" of our land called America.

Many midwestern fictionists write about the Midwest without talking of land theft and the killing of Indians and, surely, without

Indian-white colonial law. Some, like the author L. Frank Baum, a South Dakotan who wrote *The Wizard of Oz*, a lovely story about munchkins and other childish things, went further. Some of you know, of course, that he was, back in Sitting Bull's time, the editor of the *Aberdeen American News*, a northern city news organ in the Dakota Territory. He was among the media moguls of his time who advocated genocide. His editorial idea at the time of the Wounded Knee Massacre can be paraphrased as, "if we are to be safe, we must kill them all."

Does this remind you of some recent musings concerning the Middle East?

I suppose we cannot burden art with too much history or politics, but it does remind one of the responsibilities of a writer. History does have a tendency to repeat itself. For me it was something like a colleague at EWU, a German professor and writer who was writing very successful fiction about modern Germany without Hitler. It's as though the wars have been won or lost and there is no residue of hatred and violence and constant war.

Encountering my stories, then, audiences like the young girl in the front row at my reading are puzzled. Maybe I don't know how to write well enough, I chastise myself. Maybe my explications are faulty. Maybe she doesn't get irony and cynicism that many of my stories reflect. More to the point, though, maybe she has become the victim of the trend in art and literature that fiction writers in America (and their readers) are willing to cater to the idea that a convenient amnesia about our concomitant histories will win the literary prizes and the audiences, and, too often, they do. I'm asked by some American Indian literature professors who teach in English departments around the country if I feel myself a part of any particular American Indian written tradition. Of course I do, but that question does not allow me to sidestep the politics of war and death and theft and five hundred years of poisonous colonization.

The real problem is that when most Midwest fictionists do take on the real world, they become social reformers. Even Indian writers do. This means that writers are often preaching a doctrine, and that includes all of us, perpetuating the stigma attached to the indigenous populations in the Midwest, in telling the stories of failure, drunkenness, victimization, and poverty, which many people feel characterizes Indian reservation life in the middle states of the country.

Think of the professional experience of Helen Hunt Jackson in the 1820s who, as a reformer historian, wrote *A Century of Dishonor*, a remarkable text still used in general and American Indian history departments. Then, disappointingly, she wrote the fictionalized *Ramona*, which was burdened with all the history of which the author knew and despaired. The text was successful, but the novel was a commercial failure.

Today, we rarely give the legal background or the progress toward reform, and when we do we are rejected as we are thought to be "didactic," a bad word for fictionists. There is an elaborate attempt in my fictional work to overburden it with history and law. And that is why I call my effort in fiction writing self-destroying, because most literary scholars and editors simply abhor the tendency to instruct or moralize, thinking it a flaw in contemporary works.

Exposition works in soap opera and afternoon TV shows but not in the written fictional works of today, novels and poems. I've recognized that I have no talent for writing the kind of fiction that is now called modernity and often appears in the *New Yorker* or other slick magazines of the West.

It is expected that in midwestern fiction a sense of place or rugged individualism will do it: the poor, the weak, the victims, the Indians, and the land. When I am asked if I am part of any kind of Indian literary tradition, I am conflicted. I say that a Shoshone experience is not the same as a Tewa example. Or a Yakima example is not the same as the Sioux. It's not as though an Indian is an Indian, as a rose is a rose. So what is a contemporary American Indian written tradition? Those of us who have tried to exemplify that tradition know that the hardest thing to do is to be your own critic.

Lots of midwestern hard times books have sought an American audience rather successfully, and those stories seem to be part of the mainstream dialectic. I'm thinking of John Steinbeck's *Grapes of Wrath* as a model. Yet an American narrative about how some people in the West were hurt by the New Deal and then forgotten is not quite the same as the Native people (with signed treaties) hurt by the Allotment Act and forgotten, so even when one tries to find the new history with which one can imagine a novel, there is too much information missing for the average American reader. Perhaps it is just too complex, both for the author and the reader.

A particularly repugnant reality of today's literary life is that a writer must be a relentless self-promoter in order to be a part of the mainstream. That responsibility is pervasive and probably caused by economics. Public readings are a nightmare for me, especially when I recognize that I'm not thrilled by audiences who are sometimes less than receptive. I have to force myself to do readings. I once thought, before I had published anything, that readings were ego trips for the performers, who usually were, in my day at least, male poets. As an undergraduate in the 1950s I went to poetry readings of people like Robert Bly and found them to be hilarious explorations of the writer's personalities.

Since then I've learned a lot. Mostly, I've learned that a reading is an essential continuum to the art of writing itself and is a good thing. I'm still not into slam poetry and other forms of hostilities, but generally readings are a necessity for the writer to understand himself or herself and the work. There is something to be said, though, for the isolation one needs as a thoughtful writer. I like nothing more than to arrive in my little home office early in the morning. Sometimes I'm here at four o'clock, even before the sun rises. Like the Plains tipis of past times which always faced east, my study has a window that looks eastward. I do not have a drape nor a shade because the sun comes slowly and welcomes me in his own time, no other activity to be seen or heard.

It is quiet and I stare at the trees and the wide space between our house and our neighbor's for long periods, thinking my own thoughts. The huge sheltering pine trees seem to tell me not to get too far afield. To have an office or a den or a study filled with books of my own choosing is one of the luxuries of my retired life. Otherwise, in previous times, I wrote whenever and wherever I could, scattering papers here and there, hauling books up stairways, scratching notes as I drove down the road. Our old house sits on nearly three acres in a little cul-de-sac two miles out of town. In the summer our aging deck furniture shines in the hot sun and once in a while flowers bloom in two or three old pots, when I remember to water them. Wild turkeys and deer and sometimes Mr. Fox roam near the cliff and into the hills. Jackrabbits are everywhere.

I'm the self-appointed groundskeeper here, and when I get on my riding lawn mower, the little animals clear out. The Black Hills, now taken over by tourists and motorcycle jocks and complacent Christian churchgoers, was once the home of the seven bands of the Sioux Nation, where people gathered for great ceremonials. The wounds suffered by this place are heartbreaking. Somehow I am at home here.

Except for me, there are no people near my study in the early morning. CJ knew this time and place was to be shared with no one! My longings and fears and joys are my own, and the great dramas concerning the politics of being an Indian in America are dealt with here in solitude. Even a cup of coffee often waits until I'm done with this solitude.

We are bird feeders, so winter weather brings chickadees, woodpeckers, pesky squirrels, loud blue jays, a series of diverse northern larks. Few meadowlarks are here in the hills because they prefer the long prairie grasses, and I miss their songs. Few rattlesnakes live on a permanent basis in the hills, they say, but I'm not sure I believe it. Supposedly, they are prairie people, not forest types.

I wrote about the meadowlark once because I was remembering her songs, which helped me toward the audacity of writing about more personal matters, always a difficult thing for me:

The little meadowlark is the most beautiful of all birds and the
most durable. She has a yellow breast like the yellow of morning
and she wears a black necklace made from a buffalo horn. To
the Sioux her song speaks of all things in man's consciousness:
desire and love, fidelity and courage, perseverance and labor, and
strength. Because she makes her nest on the ground, her young
are constantly in danger from predators; thus, many legends tell
of her courage as a mother. Significantly, these legends say it is
her song which she uses to make herself strong. One late spring
afternoon many years ago Chunskay and I were riding with Old
Man in the wagon and I felt warm and sleepy sitting on the tail-
gate bumping along the dirt trail. I drowsed, letting my brown
stockinged legs dangle in the dust, something I would never do
in August when I thought the rattlesnakes were changing their
skins and could neither see nor hear. Chunskay was shooting
at many objects with his slingshot and the only sounds which
fell on my ears were the whiz-z-z and whir-rr-p of the pebbles
from his sling. Suddenly and without warning Chunskay "got
luck" and felled a meadowlark with his pebble; midsong, the
little bird dropped to the earth. The leather reins fell from Old
Man's hands and when I looked into his eyes I knew that there
had been another sound in the air. After that, I listened for it.
(*Then Badger Said This*, Vantage, 1977)

I see this story not so much as a personal story, which is the thrust
of most contemporary writing, as it is a legend. While much has been
made of the notion that theories of American Indian literatures are
largely dependent upon an understanding of what indigenous means
in terms of the colonial and political history of America. The events
of this story have almost nothing to do with America. It is about the
land of our ancestors, where life is real. This story could have been
told hundreds of years ago. Yet the temptation to see this as a personal story is what makes it appealing.

If we see this as legendary, though, it touches base with the legacy of a non-Christian, non-Eurocentric, and even non-Americentric literary past that is unique on this continent and asks the question: does this piece rise above personal experience, and can it, therefore, be considered a legend? The function of legend, we are told, is not only something that is handed down but something that relates to the earth, not just a place but rather a setting, a specific place. Legends happen on the earth. Myth, on the other hand, can be said to happen in the imagination or the outer world. Both are essential to complete understanding of American Indian literary expression.

In my mind, I know this place that is described in the little meadowlark story. I can take you there. It is on the Crow Creek Indian Reservation, not six miles from the home of the Old Man. Isn't that a characteristic of a legend? I think so. My grandmother used to say when she finished telling a story, "and that happened over there [pointing], on the butte . . . over there." The setting is where the meadowlark built a nest and raised a family or reproduced herself and had done so as a species for a thousand years, as the humans who hear her songs know. I can walk over there and find her nest.

Why would we think this is only a personal experience of mine, or an unverified popular story handed down from earlier times? Isn't it something more than that . . . legendary? That's the reason that when some editor from Nebraska wrote and asked me if she could use the story in a book she was writing about birds, I said yes immediately. The story is not mine.

Naturally, one must be careful about these things. *The Literary Horse* was published in 1995 by an Atlantic Monthly Press writer, and all sorts of writers from the West, including me, were solicited for stories about the horse. My story had been published before which meant that permission and acknowledgment had to be granted by someone else. There is a difference here, it seems to me, but maybe not.

It is probably important to think that the earth and the song sung by the meadowlark are traits of a legacy that maybe be different from other creatures. I think so because the Indian in the presence of these experiences becomes an essential legatee, inheritor of a legacy that is an essential postcolonial or indigenous idea, and the meadowlark is also indigenous to the western prairies, a tribal creature. The difference may be that somehow the horse belongs to everyone in the world. The Spanish! The Vikings?

Thus, to teach Native literatures is to teach them as the experiences of nations of people on this continent whose works possess nationalistic traits, not just personal ones. Pedagogy (teaching) and theory (indigenousness) must be complicit if literature is to have any usefulness or meaning. I think it is true that the worst thing colonialism did to Indians in America (and continues to do), was to obscure our past yet continue to demand that we be "authentic." The Sioux have to be horse-bound warriors, for example. Or "savages," or "primitive."

There are probably few authentic beings in this world, neither in America or Europe nor Africa or Asia. This is probably more true today than at any other time in world experience. Why should Indians, then, be expected to be authentic?

There are only indigenous beings, vis-à-vis settler and immigrant ones in the ever changing landscape of our planet. Meadowlarks are indigenous to the prairie, unlike the pheasant or the starling. Or maybe even the horse.

Let me tell you the story I just told my grandchild yesterday as we sat outside looking at the bird feeders we had just restocked with seeds and corn: "Did you know, takoja, that there are twenty million starlings in this country? They are immigrants . . . the descendants of a few dozen birds released in 1890 by the American Acclimatization Society, which was organized specifically to introduce European species to America. It was the same year that the charismatic chieftain Sitting Bull was assassinated so that other people could take over his land, to make the way for settlers."

Does this tell you something about colonization? About indigenousness? I want my Lakota/Dakota grandchildren to know what and who are the immigrants of America. Yes, I do tell my grandchildren this story because it is a wonderful metaphor to understand our own history. I hope it won't be too offensive to the readers of this gentle memoir or others who may overhear my telling of it:

> Starlings come in great numbers and then they often leave suddenly. They come in gangs, mobs, hordes chasing off the Native birds who are intimidated. Starlings, the intruders, fight all the time not only with each other, but with every other species. They are greedy and swift and are gone in an instant. . . . They will return.

For the meadowlark as for the American Indians, this history, with melancholy transience, is etched in loss.

It's not enough to teach Indian children to read and write and still use computers so that they may join the mainstream. It is not enough to teach the immigrant children to this country, whether they came in 1800 or 2010, or whether they were born to the settler class of the United States, that this country was not just known only to them. They must know that this country was possessed by indigenous peoples and prairie creatures for thousands of years.

And it still is.

For many of us history has been revealed as a catastrophe. I want desperately to share the optimism that underlies America's self-told history, but my disillusion serves as the background for all of my writing and all of my storytelling. I write that America must know who Indians are and that the homelands are sacred and that stolen lands must be returned, that there are Indians of the First Nations who possess dual citizenship in America as well as their own nations, that Indians in America are not just immature fragments of what might have been, not just symbols. They exist in the absolute, just as the meadowlark does.

We must believe in and work toward an acknowledgment of the bitter truth of our concomitant histories of vicious and mostly illegal colonization in America. America must know that the Indian in America is not on some kind of emotional and sentimental odyssey and cannot, therefore, be imaginatively possessed by anyone!

How shall I put it?

When I look at the Crazy Horse Memorial a few miles from where I live, I know that the colonial power of Euro-Americans is directed to invent their own sculpture, art, literature, and history of a Lakota man who defended his lands and people from enforced prison. When they blow up a mountain to honor him, *their action sustains the theft that killed him.*

I never take my children nor my grandchildren to see their work because I view their work as a sadistic invention used to transcend all past violence, and nothing that non-Lakota artists and historians can tell us erases the outrage of his assassination by intruders.

Our wounds give us our right to thrive in our own imaginations because we are worldly indigenous-nation people with treaties, homelands, our own heroes and resources. We are not just American identities to be imagined by others. If we want to know what the racial divide in Western America is really all about, it is that so many people in America just don't believe the Indian is in an indigenous state and always has been, with laws and memories and lives of consequence.

When I was invited recently to the University of Idaho Law School, I talked about memories and especially about law as it is known to Americans and as it is known to the latest American Indian law schools. I visited with students and teachers, booksellers, librarians, and old friends. It was a successful encounter with whites as well as Northwest Natives, and we learned a lot from our discussions.

As I got on the plane to come home, I began for the first time to accept the questions "what am I?" and "who am I?" as a quest for the totality of the species. It seemed to me to be a momentous occasion, and I went away believing that our outrage and dialogue and art, as Wole Soyinka, one of my favorite poets, has said about his African homelands thousands of miles away, must continue to provide the encounter that will assist America to become what it has said it wants to be.

At some point, I thought, America may understand its origins and its mysteries. I will continue to write and I will continue to wish it to be true that the ancestral tribal past can be accounted for in our own Indian way, in the way the Nez Perce account for it in the dictum written on the tribal blanket that was gifted me when I left their homelands and returned to mine. I thank them for that accounting.

They have given all of us the best words of tribal, indigenous thought in America, whose roots and boundaries are often distant and deep and endangered:

We did not travel here. We are of this land.
We did not declare our independence.
We have always been free.

How to reconstruct the lost Indian past expressed here is the challenge of the twenty-first century. Because I'm a survivor of the past century, I've noticed in the newest generation that the difference between Indians now and Indians then is that in response to the recognition of oppression in America toward its indigenes, restoration may not be so easy for those who do not know, remember, or think about the oldest trails.

Amnesia, perhaps, rules our present lives, and it particularly reflects the dilemmas of those who have had a brutal confrontation with colonization. The history of colonization, which is the subject of my twelfth book, probably cannot be eradicated unless those words by the Nez Perce burn in the soul of the young, not just in the aging warriors of the past.

I've noticed that many of the newest generation of educated Natives are not as interested in overthrowing the oppressor as they are in getting oppressive systems to work for them. Many Indians today are uncertain about whether or not one can diminish the importance of the European invaders' culture simply by reconstructing that indigenous mantra: *We did not travel here. . . . We are of this land.*

Yet to know the challenge is to take those words seriously as the challenge of the future. As the wounds of being survivors of the tumultuous twentieth century and previous ones are becoming more difficult to heal, the choices that must be made in order to follow the trails taken by those who came before us is also more distant and difficult. To dismantle the authority of a wrongfully told history commits us to a brilliant future rather than a desolate aftermath.

In the American Indian Lives series

Viet Cong at Wounded Knee:
The Trail of a Blackfeet Activist
By Woody Kipp

Catch Colt
By Sidner J. Larson

Alanis Obomsawin: The Vision
of a Native Filmmaker
By Randolph Lewis

Alex Posey: Creek Poet,
Journalist, and Humorist
By Daniel F. Littlefield Jr.

The Turtle's Beating Heart: One
Family's Story of Lenape Survival
By Denise Low

First to Fight
By Henry Mihesuah
Edited by Devon Abbott Mihesuah

Mourning Dove: A Salishan
Autobiography
Edited by Jay Miller

I'll Go and Do More: Annie Dodge
Wauneka, Navajo Leader and Activist
By Carolyn Niethammer

Tales of the Old Indian Territory and
Essays on the Indian Condition
By John Milton Oskison
Edited by Lionel Larré

Elias Cornelius Boudinot: A
Life on the Cherokee Border
By James W. Parins

John Rollin Ridge: His Life and Works
By James W. Parins

Singing an Indian Song: A
Biography of D'Arcy McNickle
By Dorothy R. Parker

Crashing Thunder: The Autobiography
of an American Indian
Edited by Paul Radin

Turtle Lung Woman's Granddaughter
By Delphine Red Shirt
and Lone Woman

Telling a Good One: The
Process of a Native American
Collaborative Biography
By Theodore Rios and
Kathleen Mullen Sands

William W. Warren: The Life, Letters,
and Times of an Ojibwe Leader
By Theresa M. Schenck

Sacred Feathers: The Reverend
Peter Jones (Kahkewaquonaby)
and the Mississauga Indians
By Donald B. Smith

Grandmother's Grandchild:
My Crow Indian Life
By Alma Hogan Snell
Edited by Becky Matthews
Foreword by Peter Nabokov

No One Ever Asked Me:
The World War II Memoirs
of an Omaha Indian Soldier
By Hollis D. Stabler
Edited by Victoria Smith

Blue Jacket: Warrior of the Shawnees
By John Sugden

Other works by Elizabeth Cook-Lynn

The Badger Said This
(Ye Galleon Press, 1987)

The Power of Horses and Other Stories
(Arcade, 1990)

From the River's Edge
(Arcade, 1991)

Why I Can't Read Wallace Stegner
(University of Wisconsin Press, 1996)

I Remember The Fallen Trees
(Eastern Washington University Press, 1998)

The Politics of Hallowed Ground
(University of Illinois Press, 1999)

Anti-Indianism in Modern America
(University of Illinois Press, 2001)

New Indians and Old Wars
(University of Illinois Press, 2007)

Aurelia, a Crow Creek Trilogy
(University Press of Colorado, 1999)

The Power of Horses
(University of Arizona Press, 2006)

Notebooks of Elizabeth Cook-Lynn
(University of Arizona Press, 2007)

A Separate Country; Postcoloniality and Indian Nations
(Texas Tech University Press, 2012)